AF557767

CRISIS OF SOCIALISM—
Notes in Defence of a Commitment—Vol. 6

STRUGGLE FOR SOCIALISM

Some Issues

CRISIS OF SOCIALISM—
Notes in Defence of a Commitment—Vol. 6

STRUGGLE FOR SOCIALISM

Some Issues

Randhir Singh

Struggle for Socialism—Some Issues
Randhir Singh

First Published, 2010

ISBN 978-93-5002-023-4 (Hb)

Published by
AAKAR BOOKS
28 E Pocket IV, Mayur Vihar Phase I, Delhi-110 091
Phone : 011-2279 5505 Telefax : 011-2279 5641
aakarbooks@gmail.com; www.aakarbooks.com

Printed at
Arpit Printographers, Delhi-110 032
E-mail : arpitprinto@yahoo.com

Contents

Publisher's Note

Professor Randhir Singh's *Crisis of Socialism—Notes in Defence of a Commitment* (Royal size xiii+1087 pages) was originally published by Ajanta Books International in 2006. A response to the collapse of the Soviet Union's 'actually existing socialism' and dealing with the basic issues of the why and how of this collapse, its implications and where it leaves the question of socialism in our time, the book has been hailed as a pioneering work—'one of the most important, if not *the* most important book we have ever read', 'a key to all that is going on in our world today', 'if there were a required reading list for the U.S. left, this should be on it', and so on—and there has been a persistent demand for its argument to be available in a form easier to handle and access. Therefore, with the consent of the author and in consultation with him, we at Aakar Books have decided to publish it as a thematically reorganised 6-volume edition : Volume I (Chapters 2 and 3, titled **Of Marxism and Socialism** — available in the author's *Marxism, Socialism, Indian Politics—A View from the Left,* published by us); Volume II (Prologue, Chapters 1, 4, 5, 6, 7, 8, 9, 11, 12, 13 and Epilogue, titled **What was Built and What Failed in the Soviet Union)**; Volume III (Chapters 10, 14, 15, 16, titled **The World after the Soviet Collapse)**; Volume IV (Chapters 18 and 19, titled **The Right Lesson and the Wrong Conclusion)**; Volume V (Chapter 20, titled **Contemporary Ecological Crisis—A Marxist View)**; Volume VI (Chapter 21 and 22, titled **Struggle for Socialism—Some Issues)**.

—K.K. Saxena

Preface to the Original Edition

This is a book which ought to have been published more than a decade back when its argument was first delivered as a series of lectures in memory of my friend and political associate Professor Moin Shakir at Marathwada University, Aurangabad, in February 1991. The writing naturally bears its mark but the delay has taken nothing away from the validity or relevance of my argument.

I had spoken from detailed notes and was supposed to produce a written version of these lectures. Associated with the communist movement for more than half a century, and mindful of Moin Shakir's concerns, I proceeded to write them down as a militant's response to what had happened in the Soviet Union, addressed to fellow militants in the movement and radicals at large. Part of what I wrote was published from time to time in the following years. The opening section was published in 1992 itself – in *Economic and Political Weekly* – entitled 'Crisis of Socialism – Notes in Defence of a Commitment'. This piece of writing, conveying something of my 'journey through communism' since 1939, was much noticed and appreciated at home and abroad and was reproduced and translated in many places, including an Urdu journal in Pakistan. Victor G. Kiernan, the distinguished historian, called it a 'splendid article'. Paul Sweezy and Harry Magdoff were equally appreciative. Sweezy noticed its appeal for readers of *Monthly Review* – 'many of whom (perhaps too many!) have been through similar experiences in their own lives' – and wrote to me: 'I read the piece with great interest and found it both eloquent and moving. Different as our experiences have been during the last half century, there is still much we have in common in reacting to the collapse of the revolutionary experiment in which and for which we had such high hopes'. This article soon came to be viewed as a document of the times. I have included it here as a *Prologue* to the book.

I had begun writing this draft but could not, or did not, complete it for reasons as diverse as my diffidence or lack of discipline when it comes to writing things down, more pressing or welcome academic engagements or political work, bouts of personal ill-health and, not the least, the hassles and harassments of ordinary middle class existence in the corrupt, communalised and mafiaised polity that much of India is today. The most important reason, however, was my awareness that scholars far more competent than me were writing on the subject, making it unnecessary for me to carry out the essentially secondary exercise of putting on paper what I had said at Aurangabad. And I was not wrong. We have since, for example, Istvan Meszaros' magisterial *Beyond Capital – Towards a Theory of Transition,* which has been rightly assessed as 'the definitive Marxian synthesis for the present moment, the phase of what Meszaros calls capital's *structural crisis*'. I have myself found it most useful for my argument in several places while completing these notes.

I however kept speaking on the subject or its sub-themes, discussing them with radical groups, at universities and other formal and informal gatherings; and pressure kept mounting, as much from the old-generation friends of socialism as from the new crop of young activists, that I put down my argument, such as it is, in writing. A National Fellowship at the Institute of Advanced Study, Shimla, finally persuaded me to take the plunge. But for this fellowship I would have made no progress at all with the completion of these notes. But the unexplained termination of this fellowship proved equally disruptive and delayed the completion of even this first draft by a few years. The writing is therefore obviously flawed in many ways. It bears the mark of being written, or completed, in bits, over a long period of time. That its sub-themes were the subject of separate treatment or lectures at different times or places has also contributed to uneven writing and to repetition in parts of the book. The format of Notes, with its need to provide the context of and complete the specific point being made has also added to the problem of repetition. I had expected my student and friend Arvind N. Das to take care of all this, edit and put this draft in proper shape for publication. But his premature death ruled this out. I thought of doing the needful myself, but somehow this has not been possible. In the meantime, the publication of some parts in the weekly *Mainstream* had created a constituency for what I have to say. The desirability of a better organised, more rigorously argued, and linguistically felicitous book notwithstanding, there was a growing demand that these notes be published, as they are – in their present rough form, even without references or footnotes – without any further delay. S. Balwant at the Ajanta Books International having agreed to do so, I, for myself, can only seek reader's indulgence, ask her or him to bear with the many inadequacies of this publication. What is important or really matters is its basic argument.

Occasional use of my earlier writings, particularly *Reason, Revolution and Political Theory* apart, these notes are based on my necessarily limited reading, rather what I remembered of it. I have borrowed freely from other scholars, taken their analyses as my own, used their arguments, at times in their own words, and not hesitated to quote them at length for the simple reason that they had expressed the idea or the argument better than I could have done. My debts are far too many to be acknowledged. Those familiar with the literature will easily recognise them. For me it is enough to rationalise it all by saying that these are scholars who are, so to speak, more or less on my side of the barricades.

There is one debt, however, which I would still like to explicitly acknowledge – to *Monthly Review*. It is the journal I have felt most comfortable with, intellectually and politically, over the past 50 odd years, and my debt here is writ large over several important parts of this book. For Marxist theory and sustained revolutionary commitment, there has been indeed nothing else like *Monthly Review*. Its authentic Marxist analysis of developments across the globe, easily accessible yet sophisticated in the best sense of the word, its unwavering commitment to the cause of socialism and principled support to revolutionary struggles everywhere, have educated, encouraged and inspired socialists and radicals throughout the world. Paul Sweezy and Harry Magdoff have been a constant source of enlightenment and inspiration. For me personally, Paul Sweezy was and remains a model of what a Marxist intellectual should be in our times. In recent years I have much benefited from the wide-ranging work of Ellen Meiksins Wood and John Bellamy Foster's writings in the field of ecology.

The original impulse for this writing lay in my long-time interest in understanding why and how things had gone wrong with socialism in the Soviet Union. As the crisis in Soviet society deepened in the 1980s, the subject became a matter of still more serious concern. Sometime before 'the earthquake of 1989', in my Preface to Bertell Ollman's Indian publication, *Marxism: A Uncommon Introduction*, referring to Macpherson's view that 'the utility of Marxism as a means of understanding the world is increasing over time', I had added: '"the world" includes.... not only the advanced capitalist countries or India and the so-called Third World, but the world of "actually existing socialism" also, with its troublous past, continuing problems and the truly historical predicament today'. The predicament soon ended in the ignominious collapse of Soviet socialism and then of the Soviet Union itself. But no viable Marxist explanation of what had happened was forthcoming from within the country's communist movement – a situation that still persists; even the later, more informed or updated 'official' efforts are a string of eclectic propositions: 'serious mistakes'; 'wrong notions of the role of the Party and the state'; 'the failure to effect timely changes in the economy and its management'; the failure to 'deepen socialist democracy'; 'the erosion of ideological consciousness'; etc. In this situation, as the enemies' explanation – 'socialism has failed', 'Marxism is dead', etc. – held sway, there was a demand on me to share my understanding of what had happened. The opportunity to put my ideas together for the purpose came in the form of the invitation to deliver the Moin Shakir Memorial Lectures at the Marathwada University. As originally written or rather loosely expanded or updated in many places, these lectures – my 1991 response to the interrelated set of issues involved in the collapse of the Soviet Union – constitute the core of these notes, now being published as a book.

This response is obviously not an academic exercise, a work of scholarship or historical research, and it makes no claims, absolutely none, to originality. As the sub-title indicates, my response has a strong personal dimension to it. But this does not make it merely a declaration of faith. On the contrary, what is presented here is a serious argument in behalf of the continuing validity and relevance of socialism as a historically necessary, superior-to-capitalism, social order, and the need for the common people everywhere to struggle for it. Even as each chapter stands by itself, different chapters well hold together in support of this argument. The text apart, evidence in support of my argument is there, scattered all around us, only if we are willing to see; a little reason and ability to interconnect is all that is needed.

Not an academic exercise, these are notes of a militant in the movement, 'a small "C" communist', to borrow that most helpful self-description from E.P. Thompson. And the argument is addressed to fellow militants in what is left of the communist movement, to 'social democrats' who still remain socialist, to the new crop of radicals, in the social movements or outside them, struggling to find their bearings in a world now almost universally dominated by capitalism, and to all those on the Left who share my concern with the present and future of socialism. Even others may find it of interest for their present and future too is now involved in the present and future of socialism in a way that was never the case before. If anything, these notes are an exercise in theory, a plea to parties and activists on the Left for a return to the basics. Theory, it may be added, does not directly yield a political programme which is the task of political parties or activists on the ground. But it serves to provide a basic understanding of things, a perspective or sense of direction, most necessary for the success of any popular struggle. A struggling people will not get very far without some substantial knowledge of the structures they need to overthrow for their emancipation and a sense of direction in their struggle.

[The format of Notes has enabled me to deal with a wide range of issues in this regard, many of them raised with me by the concerned activists or friends on the Left. (The chapter on Marxism, for example, in its overall thrust and detail, is very much a response to an express request from two such friends, most eminent in the fields of literature and people's theatre in Punjab). The way the original lectures were planned and delivered, there is little direct reference to India, but relevance to India is more than implicit in the argument throughout these notes. The language (English), I know, is a handicap in reaching out to a larger readership, especially at the level of activists on the ground. I hope translation will help out as has already happened with some already published parts of these notes.]

I have already regretted the repetition that marks these notes and offered an explanation, not justification, for it; though even a justification is not to be entirely ruled out. Gunter Grass has said: 'In politics you have to repeat and repeat, like a parrot, ideas you know to be correct and proven as such, which is exhausting – you constantly hear the echo of your own voice, and end up sounding like a parrot even to yourself. But this is evidently part of the job, if one is to find any listeners at all in a world so full of different voices', or, I may add, when the noisy voice of those currently dominant in society seeks to drown all other voices and wants us to forget what was said earlier and has been proved to be true, or forbids what needs to be said or repeated anew today.

If my experience with the sophisticates of the academy or bourgeois ideology, or plain anti-socialist propagandists, is any guide, 'crudeness and simplification' is a charge sure to be brought against my argument. I will not here argue or complain over it, but borrow from Marcuse to suggest that, at times, crudeness and simplification also help to make the truth of an idea more visible. And truth of the socialist idea is my main concern in these notes.

During the heady, rebel days in the late sixties, students of Paris used to ask of everyone who would address them to first tell them: 'where do you speak from?' For every speaker, and for that matter every writer, inescapably speaks or writes from a particular philosophical-political standpoint and owes it to his audience or readers to publicly state it. It is only fair to acknowledge that I have written from the standpoint of Marxism, rather Marxism as I understand it. For I have no pretensions to scholarship in Marxism. I picked up some on the way and have found it useful not only in my politics or profession as a teacher but in living my life as well. This last is not just a formal statement. Knowing Marx does make a difference to what sense you make of life, how you understand, live and act in the world. 'Indeed, I must confess that Karl Marx made a man of me', is how George Bernard Shaw once put it. Marx, therefore, is important to me and, I believe, he is important to all of us, today more so than ever before, if for no other reason than this: the world we are living in is a capitalist world, more capitalist than ever before after the Soviet collapse, and Marx more than any other human being, then or now, devoted his life to explaining the reality of this world and his achievement here remains unrivalled. In one sense, this is what this book is about.

I know that the way I have been speaking or writing about Marx, about capitalism, socialism, and such other things, in recent years, not a few have thought of me as someone woefully out of sync with our post-modern, neo-liberal or globalised times, a 'dinosaur', as it were, from another age. Many will think the same of this book and will be similarly dismissive about its argument. This is nothing to be surprised at or complain about, only something that even the best among us have to endure. Paul Sweezy and Harry Magdoff had the distinction of being referred to as 'paleolithic sectarian survivals' in the aftermath of the Soviet collapse because they continued to argue and speak up for socialism. Recently we have had the example of the Nobel Laureate Gunter Grass and the world famous sociologist Pierre

Bourdieu. Holding that neoliberalism is 'simply a return to the methods of nineteenth-century Manchester liberalism', 'a strange revolution that restores the past but presents itself as progressive, transforming regression itself into a form of progress', they have said: 'It does this so well that those who oppose it are made to appear regressive themselves. This is something we have both endured: we are readily treated as old-fashioned, "has-beens", "throwbacks"... "dinosaurs".' Grass and Bourdieu have nevertheless insisted that one must continue to speak up.

So have Paul Sweezy and Harry Magdoff, all along. Some years back, apropos post-Soviet capitalist triumphalism, they had written: 'Capitalism's victory settles nothing. In its global form, it encompasses ever more people and intensifies their exploitation and oppression. History shows that there have been alternatives in the past, and reason tells us that there will be others in the future.... It is of the greatest importance to keep the radical tradition alive and vigorous, ready to undergrid and give direction to the revolutionary struggles that lie ahead'. This is how I too had conceived this writing in 1991. Since then, the euphoria over 'capitalism's victory' long over, the struggles that lay ahead are already on the agenda of the peoples everywhere. This is where I locate whatever relevance this book has.

I would like to thank the Institute for Development and Communication, Chandigarh and its Director Dr. Pramod Kumar, for providing the facilities to complete and put together the manuscript of this book and getting the book itself into shape for the printer and publisher at Delhi. I can never be too thankful to Ashwini Kumar for the hard work he personally put into all this. I am grateful to my wife, Mohinder Kaur, for bearing with me as I struggled with this writing in Delhi, Shimla and Chandigarh. Not exactly thanks but something more is due to Priyaleen, Shimareet, Meenakshi Gopinath and Bertell Ollman who, each in her or his own way, sustained me in writing these notes. The responsibility for the argument, of course, remains mine.

Randhir Singh

March 2004

Struggle for Socialism—Some Issues

Let me conclude these notes with summing up the argument and a quick reference to a few issues of importance in the struggle for socialism which is now a matter not merely of humanity's hope for a better life on this earth but of the very survival of humanity and the earth as we have known them. That this will involve a degree of repetition is unavoidable.

The collapse of Soviet Union, whatever its other consequences, is a setback for popular struggles and liberationist projects throughout the world. Its 'actually existing socialism', a deeply deformed version of socialism as it is visualised in classical Marxism, was yet the symbol of a *possibility*, the possibility of escape from that essentially predatory system, capitalism, for the people everywhere, especially the oppressed and exploited in the third world. Also, while Soviet Union had long lost interest in any world revolutionary process, for compulsions of its own history and ideological legitimacy, national interest or *realpolitik*, or plain super-power politics, it did give some sort of aid or help to radical or revolutionary movements abroad, and provided a certain degree of support and protection when these movements emerged as revolutionary regimes. The real issue in the Cold War itself was not the aggressive or expansionist designs of the Soviet Union that needed to be confronted and foiled, as capitalism's massive hegemonic assault on the consciousness of the people of the 'free world' made it out to be. It was really a war, sometimes cold and often murderously hot, between conservative or reactionary forces, both local and external, and the peoples, notably but not exclusively in the third world, who sought a transformation of the status quo unacceptable to those forces. The collapse in Soviet Union and Eastern Europe leaves these conservative and reactionary forces everywhere that much stronger in the hope to shape the world in an image acceptable to them. Though struggle against capitalism is already back on the agenda of its victims, it is now going to be a long detour before the world returns to the task of building a more just and humane social order that is the promise of socialism. In the meantime the world will pay a heavy price for the failure of history's first effort to build socialism. The heaviest price is already being exacted by the 'victorious' capitalism under American overlordship, unrestrained in its economic, political and military arrogance now that there is no countervailing power in the world. The policies promulgated through the main agencies of global capitalism – the I.M.F., World Bank, WTO, G7 etc. – are being ruthlessly imposed upon the third and the former second worlds, seeking unrestricted movement of capital throughout the world, the deregulation and 'reform' of economies everywhere and their subordination to the dictates of global capitalism. And the overlord is on its own going about bombing and occupying nations at will and delivering 'infinite justice' in pursuit of its imperial interests.

That capitalism is 'victorious' does not mean that capitalism is not what Marxists have long proclaimed it to be, that it does not needlessly impoverish and distort the lives of millions around the globe, that it does not promote racism and national hatreds and oppressions, that it is not destroying environment faster than it can fix it, that it will not make for wars, big and small, as in the past, that it no longer holds the possibilities of nuclear and ecological disasters for humanity. 'Victorious' capitalism does not mean that its rapacious appetites will change. Rather they will only grow more rapacious, all the more so because the 'victory' has come in the midst of an unprecedented crisis of the system. A system driven by the logic of ever expanding accumulation of capital, now that it is free to expand unhindered, capitalism, damaging and dangerous as ever, will get only more damaging and dangerous. The world that is likely to emerge under the thrill of a triumphalist capitalism will be a far more unstable, iniquitous and violent world than before.

II

This world is in fact already with us as also the protest against it which suggests that struggle for socialism is back on the agenda for our times.

As Soviet socialism collapsed in the East there were euphoric declarations of 'triumph of capitalism' and promises of a new world of peace and prosperity for all. There were of course those who refused to submit to this 'capitalist triumphalism'. For them capitalism was still a system that intensifies exploitation and brings only misery and insecurity to the common people. They remained firm in their conviction that there is life beyond capitalism, that a humane and democratic society where the means of production controlled by the working people would orient production to serve the needs of society is not only necessary but also possible. But an overwhelming majority of people, including a sizeable number of erstwhile socialists succumbed to capitalism's ideological offensive that 'there is no alternative' to capitalism. 'The success of the system', Marcuse had once written, 'is to make unthinkable the possibility of alternatives'. Capitalism indeed seemed to have achieved this ultimate success, for the first time in its centuries-long existence.

The euphoria of the early post-collapse years is long over – one has to make only a simple comparison between the situation today and on the morrow of the fall of the Berlin Wall in 1989, which dramatically opened the floodgates for the so-called 'triumph of capitalism'. Capitalism's lustily proclaimed 'new world order' is increasingly recognised, and written of, as the 'great world disorder'. The hegemony of global capitalism, the legitimacy of the principles upon which its globalisation thrust is grounded, has rapidly declined in the last few years. The shortcomings and contradictions of an unregulated market economy have become more and more manifest with the passage of years. Indeed, as the eminent sociologist Pierre Bourdieu recently put it, 'the violence wrought by neoliberal policies in Europe and Latin America, and many other countries, is so great that one cannot capture it with purely conceptual analyses. Critiques of neoliberal policy are not equal to its effects'.

In the 'affluent' societies of the first world, capitalism is no longer able to maintain the old living standards, much less concede new benefits or gains to the working people. Instead, continuing a process begun a couple of decades ago, the dominant classes have been making further cuts in social spending on health and education, cutting down on employment and wages in a sharpened offensive against the welfare state as a whole. The quality of life, more fragile than ever, has steadily deteriorated in the developed nations of Europe, Japan and North America. In the erstwhile second world, face to face with the reality of capitalism, people in Russia are confronting the very issues that socialism in its original conception posed – issues of unemployment and insecurity, of poverty and inequality in society. In the third world some two-thirds (or more) of world's population continue to be kept in their condition of sub-human existence by global marketisation, or by force of arms if necessary, or, as in Africa, by the willingness of capital to let a continent die of hunger rather than change the economic system that causes it. The processes of the so-called market economy, with its stress on the primacy of private property and profit-making, are inherently anti-egalitarian. Inequalities within and between the capitalist countries have only further grown in recent years. There is a narrow and shrinking distribution of wealth and power on a world scale, their growing concentration in fewer hands which leaves rest of the world poor and marginalised. The current neo-liberal order has generated massive collapse of economies in the peripheries – in places as far apart as Mexico, East Asia, Russia and Latin America – with catastrophic consequences for the themselves-in-crisis capitalist centres and the global economy as a whole. The growing ecological crisis, the biblical migration of labour from the South and East towards the West with all its repercussions in social dumping and cultural racism, the spiral of militarisation and high-tech weapons proliferation and American actions as the super-cop of the world of global capitalism, are all posing their own intractable problems. Capitalist powers, under the U.S. overlordship, have been singularly inept and ineffective in dealing with or containing the aggressiveness and violence of national-chauvinist, religious fundamentalist, racist or fascist forces, or of what Americans prefer to describe as 'terrorism', that the failure of socialism and the success of capitalism have today generated throughout the world. Instead they are themselves generating or succumbing to such or similar forces. Nowhere in the world, including its central heartlands, is it a phase of stability, social peace and prosperity that a 'triumphant' capitalism had promised us only the other day.

It is not surprising that anti-capitalist questioning, protests and struggles have resurfaced both at the centre and in the peripheries. May be things will, or will have to, get worse before they get better. It is possible that things may get so much worse and so rapidly that humankind faces a common economic-ecological and/or military-political crisis of such alarming proportions as to constitute an absolute threat to our physical survival, moving us finally to get ourselves together and find the necessary answers before it is too late. In which case the current capitalist triumph will turn out to be only a transitory interlude. Be that as it may, it is becoming daily more clear that capitalism simply does not have the answers we need. They have to be sought elsewhere, in an alternative social system. The objective basis for a systematic search for an alternative to capitalism (and therefore for Marxism) has never been stronger than it is today. And this alternative can only be socialism. Of course socialists cannot and do not promise easy or guaranteed answers to the dilemmas that capitalism as a class-exploitative social system has created for humankind. The contention is simply that, however difficult of realisation, socialism alone carries within it the *possibility* of finding these answers.

III

Capitalism, though globally dominant and with unprecedented resources at its disposal, is everywhere failing to deliver what the great majority of the people in the world need – decent jobs, security, a livelihood worthy of human beings.

In the first world capitalism did deliver a degree of social welfare in the recent past as the 'welfare state' came up in the decades after the Second World War. This however was no structural process, something inherent in the normal evolution of capitalism. It was a contextually determined or conjunctural phenomenon, a social pact as it were between capital and labour in a particular set of historical circumstances or political conditions, which included on the one hand the threat posed by the post-war prestige of the Soviet Union, its advanced welfare programmes that competed for the allegiance of the western workers, and on the other hand capitalism's 'golden age' expansion, its cold war spending that provided the necessary resources to sustain high profits as well as growing social-welfare payments. For the capitalist class in Europe and, to a lesser degree in the United States, welfare-state social democracy was a lesser evil than communism and the extra-parliamentary left in their own countries. Not only social democrats but many others saw, even idealised it as a new goal, a mixed economy, the preferred middle ground or convergence between capitalism and socialism.

With the passage of the conjunctural circumstances or political conditions, particularly the decline and then the post-Soviet collapse disappearance of the threat from the Left, and the long term stagnation of economy which followed the crises of the 1970s, capitalist class neither needed nor could afford 'the welfare state'. Neo-liberalism that has marked the new phase of capitalist globalisation is an explicit break with the social pact between capital and labour that epitomised welfare capitalism, involving a shift from progressive to regressive taxation, from social expenditures to subsidies to corporate enterprises and, above all, a new regulatory regime which increased the mobility of capital and eliminated protective legislation for labour. The so-called middle ground between capitalism and labour has simply disappeared. With capitalism back to its normal, nineteenth-century style of functioning as an exploitative system, workers are fighting to defend their gains of the past. That is how it is with capitalism in the west today.

Social democracy has of course come up with a so-called *Third Way*, claiming it to be a new direction between capitalism and socialism. Articulated by Tony Blair in England and practised, if not preached, by the government leaders of several west-European regimes, the Third Way however is neo-liberalism implemented by people who label themselves socialists (Schroeder, Blair, Jospin, etc.), only a rhetorical gloss over a new style of right-wing politics. Building on and extending the Old Right Thatcher-Reagan doctrines of privatisation and the promotion of concentrated, centralised capital, the Third Way regimes faithfully follow the Old Right policies against labour and even exceed the Old Right in their zeal to promote the international expansion of their multinational corporations (MNCs) and banks, while admonishing labour to accept social welfare cuts and lower wages to further the competitiveness (profits) of MNCs. Even as they are failing to deliver what their own people need in terms of jobs, security and decent livelihood, the Third Way regimes have gone far beyond the Old Right in kowtowing to the U.S., and promoting Euro-American hegemonic rule over peoples of the third world. The Third Way is, locally and globally, plain and simple capitalist management of the economy, whose crisis has made any middle ground (or third way) between capitalism and socialism impossible, leaving socialism as the only possible alternative to capitalism. If the working people in the first world have any future, it lies only in socialism.

It is no different elsewhere so far as the common people are concerned, be it the Russians in the former second world, now set on the road to capitalism, but learning through hard experience the need to return to socialism, this time to socialism of Karl Marx – as the Chinese too will do before long – or peoples of the third world as a whole, with their centuries-long experience of capitalism as a global (imperialist) system. Apropos the third world, it needs to be specifically noted that the present-day misery and suffering of its peoples, an overwhelming majority of humankind, stems as much from the past and present imperialist exploitation as from their capitalistic development of the post-colonial period. It is not merely that as part of global capitalism, located in its periphery or semi-periphery, countries of the third world were seriously damaged, partly even destroyed, by capitalist expansion in the past and are now being threatened with worse economically, socially, culturally and ecologically by the ongoing globalisation. It is also that, post-decolonisation, they went on to build class exploitative societies, peripheral or semi-peripheral capitalisms of their own which, belying the hope or promises of the freedom struggle, only subjected their peoples to an additional, nationally reinforced, exploitation of the new rulers, the locally dominant classes, often in junior partnership with global capitalism.

Their 'national projects' now exhausted or abandoned, giving up the once-cherished aspiration to 'self-reliant economic development', these rulers have now opted for globalisation as their strategic option for the future. For the people, however, globalisation has meant only intensification of their ongoing exploitation. The ruling classes or elites are doing everything possible to conform to the dictates of the global market, starving and prettifying the country to compete on the 'catwalk' of attracting foreign direct investment and appeasing global capitalism as presumptive engine of country's economic development. But while national sovereignty is being further eroded, the dependent capitalism that is sought to be facilitated does not take off, and the gap with the rich nations continues to widen. Globalisation is simply failing to deliver the promised goods. The societies find themselves in perpetual crisis and the living conditions of the common people continue to worsen. The souring of the neo-liberal honeymoon that has become more of a worldwide phenomenon than might have been hoped even a few years ago, is today a part of the economic reality in the third world too. The growing opposition, especially as manifested in extra-parliamentary politics clearly suggests that alternatives have to be sought, that socialism needs to be put on the agenda of struggle in the third world, if its peoples have to avoid further peripheralisation within the global capitalist system.

This, as mentioned earlier, is not to posit socialism as achievable today or tomorrow, or even the day after, but to posit it as people's alternative strategic goal, as the principle governing people's politics which links together their immediate, ongoing and emerging struggles in an ultimate project of revolutionary transformation of society, as the goal of a long transitional process whose specifics and speed will depend on the objective material conditions and the nature and balance of class forces involved at each stage of the struggle for it. Immediately it means saying 'no' to globalisation and opting for a pro-people socialism-oriented autonomous development, one governed not by *external* imperatives, those flowing from the requirements of the world capitalist market (export-led growth, etc.) and the associated consumerism of the rich, but primarily by *internal* imperatives, those flowing from an assessment of country's own resources and the needs of its people. Development which can meet the material needs of the people in the third world is impossible within the framework of capitalism, national or globalised. Socialism has to be the strategic goal, whatever be the long or short transitional route to it. Historical experience allows no other choice.

IV

Socialism is the necessary alternative to capitalism in the world today. The fact that socialism has stumbled in some lands under some circumstances, has not changed the texture of objective reality in other lands and other times. The collapse of socialism in the Soviet Union is not the only defining moment of our times, the only epochal transformation that demands some serious 'rethinking'. Capitalism, now that it has become a truly global system, demands it even more. More free to function on its own terms than ever before, its problems and consequences too are now evident as never before. As in the past, its structural logic allows only contradictory and self-defeating solutions to problems of its own functioning. Globalisation's 'flexible' market enhances flexibility and competitiveness by undermining its own foundations as it subtracts consumers from the market. Not surprisingly, its crises, endemic as ever, are now a 'depressed continuum' spread over decades. Whatever benefits it may be bringing to a privileged minority, capitalism's consequences in deprivation and exploitation of the people, in worldwide deterioration of mass living conditions, are now all the more obvious. The failure of the much-lauded 'social' market, subject to capitalist imperatives, only underlines the impossibility of a humanised capitalism that different varieties of ideologues of capitalism keep on promising. Global dominance of capitalism has made it all the more clear that a humane and truly democratic capitalism, that staple of bourgeois propaganda, is more unrealistically utopian than the most utopian socialism. Socialism however is nothing utopian today. As a now more than ever necessary *negation* of capitalism, and with the historical experience we have, socialism is not the impossibility that ideologues of capitalism make it out to be. In the final analysis, whether we can build socialism or not, build better than in the past, depends entirely upon us, upon how the people organise and act. As Chomsky says, you act like there is no possibility of change for the better, you guarantee that there will be no change for the better. The choice is ours. Socialism is a choice we have to make and struggle for.

V

The failure of history's first experiment in socialism notwithstanding, socialism remains on the agenda of human struggle for a just and humane society. Only socialism can effectively challenge the capitalist rationality of poverty amid opulence, growth via natural destruction and the accompanying socially, morally and culturally retrograde denouements in society. Doing away with capitalism's market rationality, that governs its 'industries' of both work and leisure, socialism can put economic rationality at the service of individual and social autonomy, engaging the masses in socio-economic planning for sustainable economic development and meaningful life for all. Socialism alone has the possibility of achieving that integration of political with economic democracy, of centralised with decentralised socio-economic planning, of representative with participatory democratic structures and processes which give us the mastery of social change and conservation that we need to acquire in the decades immediately ahead if we are to secure rather than lose forever the human future. Socialism alone can enable us, humans, to have the final say on the future of not only civilisation proper but of the human species and indeed the planet – which has become a matter of such vital concern today. Against capitalism which today cannot offer anything more for the future of humanity than a diminished life in a rapidly diminishing ecosphere, socialism holds the promise of a life of rationally planned abundance with people at last gaining mastery over their lives and their world, of a more transparent and non-alienated life, which of necessity involves a reconciliation of humankind with nature, something impossible for capitalism. Such has been the emancipatory socialist project since 1848. It remains on the agenda of human struggle today.

Socialists of course have no illusions that the struggle for socialism is going to be easy or expeditiously successful. After the first failure it will be far more difficult in many ways than before, it is going to be a long detour to socialism next time. But they have no reason to feel gloomy about its prospects either. The material conditions are more favourable and objective compulsions far stronger than appeared possible a few years ago and the constituency for the socialist cause can only grow as capitalism shows itself increasingly incapable of coping with the crises it produces. Old bases of struggle among the classes and popular masses have not entirely disappeared. Old socialist and communist parties (including the reformed ones) still have some left forces and cultures for the resumed struggle of today. Militant communist formations, whatever their limitations, still survive all over the world. Popular action by diverse sections of society, expressing the desire for alternatives – not only to the neo-liberal model but also to some degree to capitalism *tout court* – has been a significant feature of the recent past: the

Chavez phenomenon in Venezuela, mass mobilisations in support of his government in defiance of the local elite and US imperialism; the indigenous people's revolts and struggles of the landless in Brazil; anti-privatisation struggles and general strikes in Bolivia; a near insurrection in Ecuador against IMF-imposed policies; continuing guerrilla war in Columbia and Peru; popular uprising and occupation of factories and sites of political power in Argentina in 2001-2002; French working-class militancy; mass strikes by workers in Italy and Germany and the Europe-wide march of the unemployed; working class actions in India, South Korea, Nigeria and South Africa; the student anti-sweatshop agitation in the United States; world-wide protests against globalisation; opposition to America's war on and occupation of Iraq and the Iraqi people's resistance, and so on. Che's legacy, the influence of 'guevarismo' lives on in the collective imagination of the fighters and in the debates about the methods, the strategies, and the nature of their struggles, as the revolutionary process in Latin America – from Nicaragua to El Salvador, from Guatemala to Mexico – enters a new phase. The Zapatista armed uprising stands as a powerful symbol of popular resistance to neo-liberal policie, not only in Mexico but in all Latin America and beyond. Latin America is in fact emerging as a particularly important zone of class struggle against international capital. Just as, far away, Nepal is another example that, odds notwithstanding, people will continue fighting for a better life.

There is a new ferment among the people, new protests and struggles everywhere, in the North as well as the South, with grievances expressed, demands made, and rights affirmed against capitalism, a growing refusal to accept the future that capitalism offers. The importance of this refusal is not to be underestimated. It provides the basis for constructing a different future, for forging the socialist alternative to capitalism. There is no denying that some of the ferment or protest does assume profoundly unhealthy forms, though, in its own muddled way, even Islamic fundamentalism can in many places become a metaphor for third world revolt against Western capitalist decadence and domination. But a good deal of this ferment and protest is progressive and speaks a language which is well in tune with socialist aspirations. This is particularly true in case of the more disadvantaged groups – women, dalits, tribals, repressed and discriminated against ethnic and other identities, etc. – now waking up to their oppressions, and of movements on such issues as women rights, racism, peace, human rights and environment. These protests and movements can hope for fulfilment only in a socialist social order. They are crying out to be articulated with the struggle for socialism.

VI

The truly global character of capitalism today, its world-wide depredations and the world people's common interest in its overthrow do constitute a material foundation as it were for a new internationalism of struggle for socialism which could draw in a huge array of progressive political forces and social interests, and which has in a way already expressed itself in the popular solidarity with the beleaguered Cuba defending its socialist gains. But politically the world continues to be a system of more or less independent states and these, therefore, remain the arena of struggle for political power necessary for carrying out a socialist transformation of society. In other words the revived struggle or struggles for socialism, as in the past, will still take place primarily within the national units of global economy and politics, without abandoning however their international concerns and commitments. It goes without saying that, again as in the past, the struggles will unfold in complicated, unpredictable ways, under the strong influence of local forces. Conditions and opportunities of struggle will be different in different parts of the world, the patterns of advance will vary greatly from one country to another, as will their models of socialism which, however, does not imply any departure from its basic principles. And as people experiment with different paths of struggle and alternate models of socialism, there will be setbacks as well as victories. In this perspective, the notion that socialism is dead says more about those who voice that notion than about future prospects of socialism. For socialists who are serious in intent, not content to live in or cry over the past or be a sermonising minority, the conditions exist to build mass support and forge new alliances, to hopefully carry on or resume the struggle for socialism.

This struggle, learning from the past, has to resolve any number of old and new problems. Even as it seeks the much-needed ideological clarity, it must reaffirm the ethical commitment of socialism. It has to challenge the established political traditions of elite conciliation and negotiations as well as cooptation of popular leaders. In a situation of deep dissatisfaction with the status-quo, with people drifting or being led into all kinds of anti-people channels, it has to seek and provide positive alternatives. The alternatives involve a new and vigorous role for the organisations of the people, especially those of the most oppressed, the worst victims of the local and global capitalism – there has to be a recognition of their autonomy, of their specific concerns and demands, independent of or in complementarity with the party or parties. It has to be a struggle from below which pushes forward the diverse emancipatory agendas of the people. The struggle will need to be specially articulated with progressive movements over strictly non-class issues and oppressions that have come up in recent decades. Given the structural nature of the transformation that socialism represents, building class and mass organisations of the working people, but shunning their economistic deformation, remains central to the politics of this ongoing or resumed struggle for socialism, as do the requisite class alliances.

To mention these considerations is not to suggest any 'model' of socialist politics. Just as there is no single or foreordained model of socialism, one that is suitable for all climes and all times, there is none of socialist politics either. As mentioned above, the specific conditions or demands and the forms of struggle they generate will vary from country to country. This, however, does not mean the absence of general principles to guide it that flow from the Marxist tradition and the experience gained in social revolutionary and national liberation struggles. These principles are implicit, or explicitly stated in different contexts, in these notes. Their recovery remains a must for any successful pursuit of socialist politics.

VII

The extraordinary diversity of the struggle for socialism in different parts of the world makes it impossible to explore its too many and too complex problems in any specific manner. I shall only make a few very general observations in this connection.

It is obviously imperative for socialists who wish for a future beyond capitalism, to understand what has happened, what was built and what has failed as socialism in the Soviet Union. They must assess the costs and consequences of this failure, the collapse of what we have described as 'actually existing socialism', and some others as 'authoritarian communism' – though they must do so fully mindful of the costs and consequences of 'actually existing capitalism' or 'authoritarian capitalism' which has rushed in to pick up the pieces. It was certainly mistaken to see the struggle for socialism in our times as a contest between 'the socialist world' and 'the capitalist world', as official Marxism of the post-1917 period made it out to be. It was, as always, an international class struggle with several more or less important fronts. The countries of 'actually existing socialism', while it lasted, were only one front of this struggle, and while they did condition or influence this struggle, positively as well as negatively, they did not determine or settle the question of its outcome. Nor does the collapse of these countries now, or their return to the capitalist fold, in any way settle the question of the future of socialism – the struggle still goes on and will, so long as capitalism lasts. Nevertheless, these countries constituted what was in many ways a most important front of the ongoing international class struggle and their collapse demands that socialists understand and come to terms with it. If they no more need to carry the burden of a deformed and degenerated socialism or be answerable for its ugliness and cruelties, the burden of a genuine, Marxist explanation of its collapse has still to be carried by them so that our people know the truth and appropriate lessons are drawn for struggles of the future.

We need this explanation not only to learn the right and not wrong lessons from what has happened, but even more because in the absence of *our* explanation, it is *their*, the enemies' explanation which will continue to prevail, and this is: 'socialism has failed'. What is more, we need it to prevent *them* from taking *our history* from us. For the ideologues of capitalism, even as they have pronounced the 'end of socialism' and with the post-modernists even deny the ability to learn from history, are busy depicting the October Revolution and what followed, an entire era of people's heroic struggles and achievements, as nothing but a costly aberration in history. Indeed, defending or reclaiming our history is today in itself a revolutionary project for us, as part of our assessment of what has happened in the Soviet Union.

An assessment or reassessment of the experience of the Soviet Union, culminating in the collapse of history's first great experiment in socialism and of the whole communist movement associated with it, even when not led or dominated by it, is obviously important for socialists everywhere, in the North as well as the South. But those who especially need to master the lessons of this experience are the leaders, and even more the militant cadre of the communist parties for whom the Soviet Union was a decisive point of reference and identity, whatever the differences that may have emerged in the later period. In the West, unable or unwilling to find answers to the Soviet collapse and related problems from within Marxism, most of these parties have simply abandoned the socialist project and opted for the social democratic road. Elsewhere, mostly in the third world, though remaining formally communist, they are confused and disoriented by what has happened, and unable to transcend the orthodoxies of official Marxism are content to blame it all on Khrushchevite revisionism, betrayal of a Gorbachev or secret machinations of U.S. imperialism and its CIA. Even the Marxist-Leninist communist formations, or those holding on to the old orthodoxies of Chinese vintage, have, by and large, failed to go beyond this much too simplistic and shallow understanding. Unless the opportunity is now seized to turn to authentic, creative Marxism to understand the crisis and collapse of Soviet socialism and this understanding made central to a rethinking of the whole question of the long current reformist or ultra-left practices in the movement, the momentum of the past may keep these communist parties going, but with the old leaders and credibility born of past struggles or gains fading out and the failure of any new radical recruitment, they can only stagnate, or continue to decline down the road of economistic practices, electoralist reforms and even pragmatic adjustments within the ongoing capitalist globalisation; and the Marxist-Leninist or Maoist formations, their avowed revolutionary commitment notwithstanding, will remain the sectarian movements they are, wrangling with each other and quarantined within their limited areas of influence. Though communist in name, these parties and formations will have lost the opportunity to recover and become a politically effective force on behalf of socialism.

For socialists in the third world, including those who call themselves communists, the Soviet experience has an added, rather exceptional importance. Classical Marxism, with its perspective of construction of socialism in advanced capitalist countries and on an international scale, had, apart from some general principles, little to say to the Russian Bolsheviks as they set out on their unanticipated journey in an entirely uncharted territory: a struggle for socialism in a single backward country, in the midst of unremitting hostility of internationally dominant capitalism led by its most advanced sectors. Theirs was a pioneering effort. Insofar as the cause of its failure lies, along with the force of objective circumstances, in the inadequacies of theory and practice for this unprecedented task, the Soviet experience has invaluable lessons for revolutionaries in the third world as, like Russia, their poor and backward countries, in this period of renewed global capitalist domination, seek a better, necessarily socialist, destiny for themselves.

As we have argued, the epoch inaugurated by the October Revolution is far from over. The first experiment in socialism has certainly failed. But it has not been a total failure. Nor does it follow that efforts to build socialism in the future will always be so constrained and thwarted. The revolutions of the twentieth century have increased our collective knowledge about how to build movements for revolutionary transformation of society as also about how and how not to build socialism. They have certainly indicated the potential for more successful future revolutions and building of socialism. The important thing now is to critically assess the current failure and the consequent crisis of socialism, to learn the necessary lessons and make it an opportunity for a more successful revolutionary politics in behalf of socialism.

The lessons to be learnt are implicit in our account above and at times they have been explicitly stated. It is not necessary to recapitulate them. I may however quote what the Italian communist Lucio Magri, in a quick overview, has to say on the subject. Speaking of 'certain notions' which marked socialism in the Eastern bloc and which have also been held in common throughout the history of the workers' movement, notions which now need to be left behind, he writes: 'These defective notions may be summarised under four headings. *Economism* identified progress with quantitative growth of (especially industrial) production, thereby underestimating other than directly economic moments and dimensions in the appraisal of individual and collective life. *Statism* overemphasised the role of centralised political power, state ownership of the means of production, and abolition of the market by decree as a lever of socialist transformation, instead of laying the stress on self-government and intellectual-moral reform in the construction of a new hegemony. *Jacobinism* separated off the Party, as enlightened vanguard, from the masses, and thus entailed a bureaucratic organisational form of the party itself. *Eurocentrism* involved the idea that the Western model could be extended world-wide, defining the social subjects and cultures of other peoples in terms of underdevelopment and reducing them to the rank of mere allies. This whole complex of mentalities helped to produce degeneration in societies where a revolution was accomplished, but it has also hindered the Western Left from uniting with Third World movements and from mobilising the new social subjects that are emerging under advanced capitalism.' This is not an altogether adequate assessment, but it is certainly worth emphasising that the most important lesson here concerns 'economism' which not only came to characterise the construction of socialism in the Soviet Union but has also generally dominated the ideology of communist parties and radical workers' and people's movements outside, in both the advanced and underdeveloped countries. The Soviet experience shows most clearly where economism heads and the analysis of this experience thus constitutes an indispensable 'negative lesson' for those who want to struggle for socialism while ridding themselves of economism in their theory and practice.

The lessons, often bitter ones, have to be drawn from the past. This is necessary to face reality and rebuild the required politics and culture on the left. But it is equally necessary to be properly balanced about it. In other words, it also needs to be recognised that this past is not entirely a bitter heritage. 'Historical communism' as it has been called, the outcome of October Revolution including the Soviet experiment, has extraordinary achievements to its credit. We have taken note of them in the foregoing pages. As with lessons, there is no need to recapitulate them either. Behind these achievements lie heroic sacrifices of generations of communists and the people led by them, and a wealth of revolutionary theory and practice, implicit in a long record of peoples mobilised, movements built, struggles waged, battles fought and won, revolutions made and entire societies transformed, and explicit in the writings of Lenin and Mao, Ho Chi Minh and Che Guevara, Rosa Luxemburg, Trotsky and Gramsci, and a host of other revolutionary leaders and thinkers in different parts of the world. All this is our asset for struggles in the new period. As we look at this new period, there is one achievement that I would still like to recapitulate. To quote from the Prologue:

> Indeed, without the 'historical communism' as it has been called, this world of ours would have been a far more inhuman and hopeless place. Beyond its historically specific achievements... is a somewhat intangible aspect of the social reality around us today, a general illumination, as it were, that bathes all the failed and successful peculiarities of our age. You have to take only one, quick look around to recognise the living presence of 'historical communism' in the enhanced awareness of humankind the world over concerning issues of human dignity, of justice and injustice,

> of equality, oppression and exploitation, in the voice and hope the poor and oppressed have come to acquire in our times, in the quality and spread of their struggles for a better life and, above all, in their confidence, despite all the retreats and reverses, that they can fight and win their emancipation...

As Rene Depestre has pointed out 'communism' tried for the first time in history, at least as never before, to link thought and action, forging links between the intellectual, worker and peasant. Not only that, it brought them centre-stage in history and changed social thought and reality most significantly in favour of the common man. The Soviet experiment may have failed but, recent disillusionment among certain sections notwithstanding, the idea of socialism has caught on, especially with the poor and oppressed of the world, that no failures can now efface. Beneath the socialist idea are a core of egalitarian values: the human right to creative, productive work; the right to accessible and dependable health care; the right to decent housing; the right to public education; freedom from oppression based on race, gender or ethnicity; the elimination of great concentrations of wealth, power and privilege in the hands of a tiny minority; the democratic empowerment of those who historically have experienced the burden of exploitation and oppression. These values have now come to stay, not as something to be only cherished but as a distinct possibility in our times. The record of even advanced capitalism on all this only reinforces the belief that the socialist alternative continues to be both relevant and politically necessary. On balance the communist-led revolutions of the twentieth century have weakened the reign of capital and enhanced the possibility of moving towards socialism as Marx visualised it, to which democracy, it needs to be re-emphasised, is a central concern. Among other things they effectively challenged the sacredness of private property. Common ownership of the means of production, despite bureaucratic usurpation in the Soviet Union, has come to be associated with values of solidarity, security and egalitarianism. These revolutions have certainly left capitalism more vulnerable to the next wave of revolutions in the world.

The reference to 'common ownership' allows me to make another substantive point regarding the need to be properly balanced in our assessment and assimilation of what has happened in the Soviet Union. There has been a tendency that in refusing to be 'nostalgic for the command economy', or seeking to 'reinvest in democracy at all levels if the left wants to speak of planning once again', or otherwise drawing the long overdue attention to the centrality of democratisation in the process of socialist construction, the importance of public or common ownership is underplayed or lost sight of. This is a grievous mistake. A *genuinely* public or common ownership of the means of production is an absolutely indispensable foundation for a social order radically different from capitalism. For this alone makes society-wide planning and conscious decisions about the overall use of resources possible. It may be added, public ownership is not synonymous with state ownership; it can and must assume many different forms, from *socialist* state's ownership of the commanding heights of the economy to municipal and cooperative ownership. Nor need public or social ownership, even in its different forms, be all-encompassing. A private sector, with a multitude of small-scale enterprises, catering to a variety of needs could continue to exist alongside the public sector, certainly so during the long or short transitional periods. The point about this transitional 'mixed economy' is that the public sector should decisively outweigh the private one so that effective overall planning, democratically central and decentralised, is possible and on the whole not 'market' but politics, that is, revolutionary socialist politics, remains in command of the economy, ensuring that people's interests retain their priority and the general direction of the socialist advance is maintained. (In the same way, socialism continues to stand for the abolition of commodity production. But this does not mean that the market will vanish immediately. It only indicates the general direction of advance that needs to be secured during the long or short transitional period). I have made this digression not merely to clarify an issue of cardinal importance in socialism that is being lost in the current retreat from or confusion about socialism, but also suggest that the resumed struggle for socialism needs to repossess itself of its traditional foundations and not turn its back on them under pressure from capitalism's ideological offensive that has followed the collapse of Soviet socialism. Our critical assessment of this collapse must not involve any 'rethinking' that abandons the very principles of socialism.

For socialism to have any future, the movement for it needs to make a critical assessment of its past, indeed not only after the October Revolution but also seventy years before it to know where it has come from and what it aims at, know not only the resources it lacks but also the ones it has. Its self-accounting has to be a proper one which does not throw any baby out with the bathwater, but remaining careful of its basic principles critically appropriates its past or heritage for the tasks of the present. Making a mess of this past or heritage in any manner, apart from being poor politics, is an evasion of the responsibility, of the elementary care and sense of proportion which each generation of revolutionaries owes to the efforts of generations of revolutionaries before it.

Before leaving this subject, I would like to point out that failures and defeats are not unexpected or unknown in the tradition of classical Marxism. The defeat of 1848 revolutions, the end of the Communist League, the destruction of the Paris Commune, and all sorts of failures were part of the experience of Marx and Engels as revolutionaries. But, taking a proper, historical view of it all, they carried on with their theoretical and practical work in the cause of socialism. Defeats and failures were studied and analysed to prepare a path for renewed struggle. It was via their close analysis and criticism of the revolutions of the 19th century that the dynamic of Marxism-led revolutions of the 20th century was arrived at. And of proletarian revolutions themselves Marx had pointed out that they go forward by constantly criticising themselves; prodigious in their aims, they are obliged continually to interrupt themselves, to turn upo their own inadequacies and flawed earlier attempts, in a process of relentless self-criticism. 'Proletarian revolutions', wrote Marx in *Eighteenth Brumaire*, 'criticise themselves constantly, interrupt themselves continually in their own course, come back to the apparently accomplished in order to begin it afresh, deride with unmerciful thoroughness the inadequacies, weaknesses and paltrinesses of their first attempts, seem to throw down their adversary only in order that he may draw new strength from the earth and rise again, more gigantic, before them, recoil ever and anon from the indefinite prodigiousness of their own aims, until a situation has been created which makes all turning back impossible, and the conditions themselves cry out: *Hic Rhodus, hic salta! – Here is the rose, dance here!'*

Facing the unanticipated and unprecedented task in Russia, Lenin did not discount the possibility of 'defeat', in which case he had hoped the 'experience will benefit other revolutions'.

Perhaps the clearest expression of the revolutionary Marxist perspective here is to be found in Rosa Luxemburg: 'No pre-established schema, no ritual that holds good at all times, shows (the proletariat) the path that it must travel. Historical experience is its only teacher; its Via Dolorosa to self-liberation is covered not only with immeasurable suffering, but with countless mistakes. The goal of its journey, its final liberation, depends... on whether it understands that it must learn from its own mistakes. Self-criticism, cruel unsparing criticism that goes to the very root of things is life and light for the proletarian movement.' There is no other school of political maturity available to working people thn the experience of struggling for power, now failing, eventually succeeding: 'The final victory can be prepared only by a series of "defeats"'. Addressing as if our own post-Soviet collapse times, Rosa Luxemburg wrote: 'We are truly like the Jews whom Moses led through the desert. But we are not lost, and we will be victorious if we have not forgotten how to learn.'

But as we thus learn from the failure in the Soviet Union, it is imperative to remember and insist that the epoch inaugurated by the Russian Revolution of 1917 is not over. 'Great revolutions', as Meszaros has said, 'reverberate over centuries, until their underlying causes are resolved.... they are best compared to monumental earthquakes. The mountain ranges they bring to surface cannot be undone and pushed back into the earth's belly'. It is foolish of our opponents to try to bury the October Revolution just because of what has now happened in its place of origin. It was a revolution with socialist aspirations which cannot be wiped out of history. Its was a powerful vision that has motivated, and continues to motivate, millions. The failure in the Soviet Union is not the death of a tradition of revolutionary theory and practice, of struggle for socialism. It is only that henceforth others are destined to carry it forward. Socialism will find newer and better standard bearers and protagonists than the Stalinised and semi-Stalinised states or movements of the past. The struggle, at any rate, will continue.

VIII

As we come to terms with the collapse in the Soviet Union and the struggle for socialism is resumed, Marx's critique of capitalism remains central to the socialist project. That capitalism, now that it is universal and has therefore also become virtually invisible and disappeared from the public discourse does not change the reality of things, only makes it all the more necessary to recognise it for what it really is, that is, capitalism which has made socialism both necessary and possible today.

The centrality of Marx's critique of capitalism for the socialist project can never be overemphasised, whatever be the specific character of capitalism or capitalist domination in a country and notwithstanding capitalism's remarkable resilience in surviving, which resilience we have noticed on more than one occasion earlier and which any serious struggle against capitalism must take note of. It was Marx's radical critique of the prevailing social order, of capitalism as a system structured by contradictions which are insoluble in its own terms, that led him to affirm that an entirely different social order, based on radically different foundations is not only desirable (which is easy enough) but possible. The socialist project depended not on the appeal of a theory but on the reality and power of contradictions, tendencies and possibilities that the theory correctly identified within capitalism, on Marx's analysis and prognosis of the inner logic of capital, which analysis and prognosis stands fully vindicated by the development of capitalism over four centuries. The critique of capitalism was indeed the starting point of Marxism and socialism and is the point to which, quite properly, the socialist movement can and must now turn.

This critique alone prevents Marxism from being obsolete at least while capitalism lasts. In reply to the question, 'Is Marxism obsolete?' Issac Deutscher had suggested precisely this and drawn attention to capitalism's basic contradiction that Marxism had revealed: 'There is one, only one essential element in the Marxist critique of capitalism. It is very simple and very plain, but in it are focused all the many-faceted analyses of the capitalist order. It is this: there is a striking contradiction between the increasingly social character of the process of production and the anti-social character of capitalist property... an anti-social kind of property, private property. This contradiction... is the source of all anarchy and irrationality in capitalism.'

The *capitalist* private property is specifically anti-social because of its exclusive pursuit of profit-making and accumulation regardless of the consequences. If the main structural weakness of capitalism lies in its inability to ensure this as a smooth, uninterrupted process which inability finds expression in periodic crises of profitability, of investment and of economic activity in general, its social or moral weakness lies in the fact that its pursuit of profit and accumulation inevitably has disastrously damaging consequences for the vast majority of humankind. These consequences, the widely acknowledged economic, social, political, moral and ecological failings of the system must not be viewed as unfortunate deviations from its normal working, they are on the contrary an intrinsic outcome of the structural logic of capitalism. It is the attenuation of these damaging consequences by way of public intervention or regulation which must be taken as deviations from the essential dynamic of capitalism, as contrary to its spirit and purpose, which intervention or regulation capitalism has always opposed, evaded or sought to shake off at the first opportunity. It is important to note that the liberal or social democratic critiques of capitalism have typically tended to be piecemeal and specifically related to immediate 'problems', shortcomings and failings of the system. Criticism is directed at one aspect or another of the social order dominated by capitalism, without this criticism being related to the nature of the system as a whole. A Marxist critique, with its dialectical orientation, recognises and establishes the connections that exist between specific ills and the nature of capitalism as a system wholly geared to the pursuit of private profit, whose dynamic and ethos suffuse the whole social order, and which necessarily relegates all considerations other than the maximisation of private profit to a subsidiary place, at best, in the scheme of things. Important from the point of social and political analysis and even more of the struggle against capitalism is the polarisation in society that capitalism necessarily gives rise to and which capitalistic hegemonic endeavours constantly seek to befog or deny. To put it simply, capitalist societies are fundamentally divided between, on the one hand, dominant classes so defined by virtue of their ownership or control of the main means of domination – the means of production, the means of administration and coercion, i.e. the state, and the means of persuasion and consent – and, on the other hand subordinate classes, so defined by virtue of their relative (or absolute) lack of ownership or control of these means. The interests of these classes are fundamentally divergent and the result is a permanent struggle between them, which hidden or open, assumes many different forms at different times but which is inherent in capitalism as in all preceding societies based on domination and exploitation. The struggle for socialism is the highest form of self-conscious emancipatory struggle of the subordinate classes today.

Marx's critique of capitalism and the associated insights have lost none of their power and relevance, but they need to be fleshed out and applied in the new conditions, on a global scale and in relation to the historical specificities of the situation in different countries. It is of course important to know how precisely the logic of late capitalism is at work in the advanced capitalist countries of the world, where mass unemployment, great inequalities in all spheres of life, material constraints of all kinds, moral and cultural disorientation, widespread sense of spiritual want, anomie and alienation are a lived reality for vast masses of people today. But it is equally and in some ways perhaps more important to focus on the complex set of interactions between the so-called 'first' and 'third' worlds where, with the ongoing globalisation and imposed 'structural adjustment', the basic relationship of exploitation – backed where necessary with military power – has assumed a still grosser form of the transfer of resources from the poorest people on earth to the richest, *and* on the situation within the third world countries themselves where, the collaborating native exploiting classes are content with their share of the loot, and the people – their countries increasingly locked into the global capitalist system and helpless in the face of its logic – face the prospect of further impoverishment, mass deprivation and hunger. And all this when resources produced by 'social labour' under capitalism itself are available that make possible decent livelihood and a life of dignity for all on this earth.

It is not only that Marx's critique of capitalism remains relevant, providing the requisite knowledge for a worldwide renewal of struggle for socialism, the terrain for this struggle too is not as unfavourable as is generally presumed. The structural logic of capitalism is visible as never before and people's experience of capitalist exploitation and domination is only being accentuated by the current crisis of capitalism. With this crisis and the decline of revolutionary opposition, the prerogatives of capitalism are being reasserted with increasing cynicism, at the centre through 'restructuring' of the economy, union-busting and dismantling of the welfare state, and in the periphery through globalisation which, in collaboration with the local ruling classes, makes for reinforced exploitation of the poor and oppressed of the third world. This capitalist offensive is helping the common people everywhere to see more clearly the real face of capitalism. At the same time some at least of the ideological props of capitalism are gone, certainly those provided by the cold war and the authoritarian Soviet system. Anti-communism was a powerful weapon in the hands of the capitalist ruling classes to assert their class power. The loss of the old 'enemy' is proving painful to the capitalist power-brokers and profiteers, the new 'enemies' being discovered --'Islamic fundamentalism', 'terrorism', the so-called 'rogue states', etc. – are rather poor substitutes for it. With capitalism's new offensive against the working people undermining its legitimacy, and some of the ideological props gone, the abuses of the capitalist system are more difficult to mask and those criticising its irrationalities harder to silence. The discrepancy between the high rhetoric of capitalist apologetics – about freedom and democracy, fairness and equal opportunity, justice and common interest, 'development with a human face', prosperity for all, etc. – and the reality as it is daily experienced by the vast majority of people under capitalism stands more clearly revealed, threatening the fragile structures of bourgeois hegemony over society. And the way things are going it may not be long before people come to recognise the ugly face of capitalism in the looming environmental crisis. All this surely provides a terrain increasingly favourable to renewal of argument and struggle for socialism.

It was distinctive of Marx's critique to simultaneously recognise capitalism's extraordinary productive achievements and its structurally-ordained inability to use them for universal human welfare. It saw these achievements as providing the objective, material basis for socialism as the system which can secure such welfare, and underlined working people's capability to overcome capitalism and build a socialist society. That a socialist society is both necessary and possible emerges more directly out of Marx's critique of capitalism today than ever before. Lucio Magri has written:

> For the first time, humanity has the resources and productive capacity to assure the satisfaction of basic needs and a minimum of civilization for all. And yet, a growing part of humanity – whole peoples and continents in the South, but also a not insignificant part of the affluent metropolis – are enduring old and new forms of poverty, fighting and often losing the battle for sheer survival.
>
> For the first time, humanity is running up against the limits of natural resources. It has the scientific and technological means to husband those resources and to pursue greater well-being

through improvements in the quality of life rather than senseless growth in the quantity of material goods. But the dissipation of nature is continuing, in some sectors actually accelerating, and with it a model of life that promises disasters in the future and is already undermining human welfare.

For the first time, at least in the North, consumption levels have passed the threshold of natural need, they now allow both for the real enrichment of distinctively human consumption and for the satisfaction of remaining needs. Instead, however, the repetitive, imitative and depersonalized character of consumption is becoming more marked, without either satisfying existing needs or creating higher ones.

For the first time, as a result of the scope and pace of technological innovation, it is becoming possible and almost obligatory to reduce the sum total of necessary human labour and to set greater store by its quality. And yet, the reduction in necessary labour is translated into structural unemployment, and an even greater separation is made between stable, skilled labour and insecure, fragmentary, alienating tasks.

For the first time, education and rapid communication offer the means for a general rise in culture and critical awareness, which are in turn the basis for any real democracy. Yet they are turning into instruments of manipulation, of a conformist common sense, disorienting the masses and rendering them passive.

For the first time, then, modernity and progress do not appear as synonymous of civilisation and equality, however uneven or gradual in their development, but are threatening to open the way to a caste society and general barbarism...

IX

'Without a revolutionary theory', Lenin had rightly insisted, 'there can be no revolutionary movement.' While resources from other, especially native radical traditions are always important, Marxism remains theoretically basic for all genuine anti-systemic movements today, above all for the now more than ever necessary struggle for socialism.

As we have argued, so long as capitalism exists, socialism, which is its anti-thesis, remains on the agenda, however long be the haul for it. It is no coincidence that within a decade of the collapse in the Soviet Union and the accompanying proclamations of 'the death of socialism', capitalist societies everywhere are in deep economic and social crisis, crisis and contradictions of capitalism, its globalised depredations, are at the centre of popular concern and there is a renewed search for an alternative. Anti-capitalist struggles have surfaced and any number of new movements have come up whose aspirations can be realised only in socialism. But evidence indicates that without an organised theory, and practice based on it, they will have surfaced and come up only to be frustrated and defeated, lending legitimacy to the claim that 'there is no alternative' to the present order. To be successful, even for their limited aims and purposes, they need a theory which enables them to see the interconnections of their particular concerns with the social reality as a whole and provides them with a viable strategic alternative. Marxism is the theory they need. This apart, what we confront today is a capitalism that has acquired universal domination and monopolised the discourse and ideology of our era. To confront it successfully we need alternative modes of thinking and acting that are universal and global, and which confront the system and its worship of money and the market in a thoroughly radical fashion. Nothing better qualifies as the needed alternative way of thinking and acting for our times than Marxism, providing as it does not only the 'framework for radical criticism aimed at a fundamental restructuring of society in its entirety' as Istvan Meszaros has argued, but also a rich legacy of socialist politics, its strategy and tactics, born of more than a century of worldwide revolutionary struggles under its banner.

Despite all talk of 'failure' or 'crisis of Marxism', Marxism remains the necessary theory for the new phase of struggle against capitalism. This makes a new revival of Marxism certain. But the 'crisis of socialism' demands that this revival needs to be a *renewal* of Marxism, a recovery of 'Marxism of Karl Marx' as I have described it.

As I understand it, it is Marxist to insist that Marxism needs a renewal in the light of our historical experience. It has to come to terms with large, formidable questions, many of them left unraised or unanswered, or found impossible of answer by those gone before us. There are the obvious questions arising from the failure of the first experiment in socialism. This failure has made it abundantly clear that the construction of a new, socialist society is far more difficult than it was ever visualised. Answers have to be found to any number of important questions involved in this construction, indeed in any transition to socialism, such as how to ensure genuine social ownership and popular participation in and control over the economy, how to secure democracy in society, combining its representative and direct forms, how to articulate democratic planning with the inevitable, if necessary, relics of the market, how to reconcile economic growth with ecological imperatives, and so on. Insofar as backwardness of Russia was an important factor in accentuating the unresolved problems of this transition, they are bound to recur as revolutions again unfold in the third world.

The failure in Russia in fact reopens as never before the entire question of what is to be the overall perspective of struggle for socialism in the more or less backward, peripheral capitalist countries of the third world in a situation of global domination of capitalism. But it is not only in the third world that the struggle for socialism faces new problems. The struggle in the first world too faces parallel problems of its own, many of them accentuated by its 'overdevelopment' so to speak, and by the latest phase of globalisation. Indeed, world over the struggle for socialism faces new and old, unresolved problems which are crying out for a creative Marxist response. They have to be honestly recognised and resolved through an open and pluralistic debate within and without the parties and formations committed to socialism. No one, no person, organisation or party can claim to have a monopoly over truth in this matter, certainly not in the name of any 'science of Marxism'. Many of these problems have been noticed and dealt with in different contexts in the preceding chapters. Before discussing some of them more specifically, I would like to touch upon a few issues of general, theoretical nature that renewal of Marxism today involves.

It needs to be recognised that the legacy of the past, along with its gains, has also left behind quite a few problems that renewal of Marxism today has to address. Immediately noticeable here are the falsifications and distortions of the Moscow-backed 'official Marxism' that acquired the status of orthodoxy in the Communist movement. The collapse of the Soviet Union of course has its advantages for the revolutionary communists. There is no so-called 'Party of Lenin' now to mislead them or subordinate the communist movements abroad to the requirements of Soviet foreign policy, the 'national interests' or *raison d'etat* of the Soviet Union. Nor any longer those parodies of Marxism and the accompanying pseudo-internationalism that, in one way or another, for generations, divided, disoriented and emasculated communists and socialists throughout the world. The new situation leaves them free, after a long time, for a bold and confident, truly innovative and non-sectarian practice of Marxism. But this is only if they want to. For the fact is that 'official Marxism' (along with a parallel orthodoxy in the name of Mao) continues to dominate in what is left of the old communist movement. Marxism often stands reduced to an 'honorific' word to be used at ceremonial occasions or political festivities at home or at international conferences with their declarations of the 'invincibility of the science of Marxism – Leninism', occasionally along with 'Mao Tse-tung Thought' too! The need for rectification, for a return to Marxism of Marx is obvious.

Marxism has always had an extraordinary potential for critical and subversive thought and action. It not only gave rise to a massive worldwide movement that has ebbed and flowed over the last century and a half, with its victories and defeats, shared by all of us, and often bitter conflicts among revolutionaries. But as the main revolutionary force in the world, it also became the natural gravitational centre for movements of all kinds that sought to remedy poverty, fight national oppression, protest social injustice or express outrage at the manipulation of humanity by the powers that be, and so on. Thus cult-like alienated groups, terrorist organisations, liberation armies and the like, all rallied to the banner of Marxism and used its vocabulary to express their demands and aspirations, creating problems of a different kind within or around Marxism. In other words, the very success of Marx's ideas, of whatever kind, as the inspiration for small, often sectarian groups or formations, mass political movements, and even successful revolutions, has led to all sorts of mistaken systematisation, rigidities and distortions that a renewal of Marxism has to take care of and overcome. Marxism, of course, has the resources within itself to do so.

Looking at it from the other end, much the same can be said about the need to retrieve Marxism from the deluge of 'theoretic' writing, the flourishing 'Marx industry' in the West – another penalty paid by Marxism for the 'success' of Marx's ideas.

Marxism has not been immune to ideological deformation of another kind which needs to be specifically noticed. It treats Marxism as an all-purpose talisman, so that instead of being used for the methodological investigation of reality through theory and practice, it is misused as a defence against that very reality, digging in behind stereotyped, simply affirmative dogmas or exorcisms, overarching, essentially irrefutable, abstract or holistic references to total situation, without any serious recognition of its manifold mediations. It is forgotten that there is always the need for a 'concrete analysis of concrete conditions' as Lenin put it, for a precise analysis of the exact causes which makes possible – of course within a framework of general theory and in full awareness of the ultimate objectives – specific intervention, here and now. In the absence of such analysis, and action based on it, even advocacy of revolution can become an empty formula, the ideological mask of passivity. Marxism demands a continuous engagement with social reality, every aspect of it, if we would change this reality.

What is involved in these and other specific issues of the renewal of Marxism is a demand for returning to the authentic tradition of revolutionary Marxism, returning to Marx and Engels and best of their followers in a self-critical spirit, bearing in mind the context of what they said and did and relating their analyses, ideas and actions to the milieu we are in. The current crisis of socialism not only demands but is really the occasion for such a return, for a rebirth of critical thought within Marxism, calling into question all the received dogmas, restoring to

Marxism its original subversive power. It is the opportunity to renew Marxism as a theory which, liberated from the nostalgic orthodoxies of the past, be they of Soviet, Chinese or any other vintage, and declining quoted guidance from one Marxist authority or another, draws upon the *entire* exceptionally rich, revolutionary tradition of Marxism, including those currents within it which, reflecting its more humane and democratic dimensions yet remained marginal, unable either to achieve adequate theoretical expression or to produce an effective politics. Humanism and democracy lie at the very core of Marxism, making it a truly revolutionary doctrine. Marxism needs to recover its much-neglected humanist and democratic heritage. It is an aspect of the ongoing ideological class struggle that, as for example with the work of Luxemburg and Gramsci, this heritage is being interpreted and appropriated by the enemy for reformist and even counter-revolutionary purposes. As we have already noticed, since the 'discovery' of the powerful humanist theme in Karl Marx, even he has not been immune to such vulgarisation of his theory.

Marxism has to be so renewed that rejecting the post-modernist apologies for the established order, the 'realistic' discourse legitimising the capitalist market or the social-democratic surrender to it, it develops to a level adequate to the reality of the contemporary world. It has to be a Marxism which is not content with self-assuring declarations of faith, restatements of its perspectives in the abstract or assertion of the *ultimate* validity of its cause, but is willing and able to engage with every concrete problem in society and offer alternatives, able to integrate, in the words of Istvan Meszaros, 'the totality of social demands, from the most immediate "non-socialist" everyday concerns to those openly questioning capital's social order as such, into a theoretically coherent as well as instrumentally/organisationally viable strategic alternative.' World-wide, new forms of popular struggles and movements, new liberationist currents – liberation theology, ecologism, feminism, pacifism, struggle for human rights and struggles of ethnic and other identities – are emerging, even if most of them do not yet see their connection with the irrationality and manifold oppressions of capitalism. Our Marxism, actively positive in its attitude to the emerging popular struggles and movements, and liberationist currents, needs to be able to deepen their understanding of things and articulate them with the struggle for the strategic goal of socialism.

Most important in any renewal of Marxism today is an active return to a principle which is basic to Marxism of Marx. 'Think for myself' was a general remark made by Kant which Marx had taken for himself. So must we 'think for ourselves'. That the situation today is one almost entirely unanticipated by classical Marxism makes it all the more imperative for us to do so, which in effect means we have to 'think as Marx would have thought in our place'. Engels had insisted that 'it was only in that sense that the word Marxist had any *raison d'etre*'.

The situation today also demands that our Marxism needs to have the quality that distinguished Marxism of Karl Marx: an uncompromising hostility to the system of exploitation that is capitalism. In other words, what is needed today is a fiercely combative Marxism, a socialist combativity towards capitalism, the system that is sought to be challenged. The traditional communist parties, whatever their other faults, once embodied this quality, later dissipated by decades of reformist theory and practice, often under Soviet inspiration or leadership. They simply lost the habit of thinking in fundamentally anti-capitalist ways. What is most marked about them now is not so much their greater willingness to be critical of the Soviet past, but, like most others on the Left, their lack of any radical hostility to capitalism itself. An essential precondition for the emerging struggles on the Left to become a viable force for socialism is a recovery of this hostility, a single-minded and determined position on the necessity of a rebellion against and categorical rejection of the day's conventional wisdom of 'there is no alternative'. Socialism remains the alternative. But for socialism to have a future, among other things, there has to be a return to the revolutionary intransigence of a Marx or Lenin, Mao or Che Guevara.

X

If there is the need for proper self-accounting to retain or recover the resources that the socialist heritage still provides, it is equally necessary to recover our vision of the future, much dimmed by developments of recent years. One residual consequence of the Soviet collapse is a sudden inhibition of social imagination. The present world-wide triumph of neo-liberalism and the accompanying spread of bourgeois values (including the 'American way of life'), resulting from the failure of both Soviet socialism and Social Democracy in the west to offer a significant, that is both a radical and democratic, alternative to the world capitalist system, has caused a precipitative retreat from the ideal or vision of socialism itself. Much that was positive and necessary is being abandoned: a commitment to social justice, equality, internationalism, solidarity or struggles and so on. The assertion of a need to intervene and plan and direct economic activity is rejected when the cosmic destructiveness of the capitalist market economy has never been more evident. Globalisation is accepted or helplessly endorsed when the new world order of capitalism is so obviously based on yawning inequality, virulent strains of racial conceit, high-tech militarism and unprecedented threats to the habitability of the planet. In the prevailing climate of 'there is no alternative', the Left, inevitably influenced by the beliefs of those around it, is accepting parts of their agendas and adopting their vocabularies, or resisting this pressure by retreating into fortress dogmatism, which in practice has the same consequence. In the *Kulturkampf* that is now on all over the world, as capitalism is offered, accepted or imposed as the ultimate horizon – often under such deceptive labels as liberalisation, economic reform, structural adjustment, industrialisation, even democracy – the socialist horizon has been shrinking. There is a lowering of sights, a loss of focus on the priorities and values that mark the socialist/ communist project as revolutionary and worthwhile. Ironically, a pessimism not only of the intellect but also of the will seems to have taken hold. The Left as a whole has gone on the defensive – and defensiveness has tended to squelch the visionary, 'utopian' dimension of socialist thought and practice.

The consequence is that even as the parties of the Left pursue their inherited reformist programmes – these are by no means wholly useless and will always precariously survive, to a greater or lesser extent, through popular support, even within today's capitalism – the political project as a whole is ever more stuck in daily tactics, ever more inspired by the 'art of the possible', and the so-called 'ground realities', and therefore disposed to compromises. Competition on the terrain of bourgeois politics necessarily produces electoral stagnation or decline, and at a more fundamental level, decline in the activity, enthusiasm and social embeddedness of their supporters. The experience inevitably deluding the expectations, the result is an overall tiredness and ennui, scepticism and depoliticisation, within and without the parties, until people can no longer distinguish between the left and the right.

Towards the end of *What is To Be Done*? – a text which is as relevant today as ever, Lenin, in the midst of the most hard-headed and unsentimental of polemics, quoted the journalist Pisarev: 'if man were completely deprived of the ability to dream... if he could not from time to time run ahead and mentally conceive... the product to which his hands are only just beginning to lend shape, then I cannot at all imagine what stimulus there would be... [for] art, science, and political endeavour... The rift between reality and dreams causes no harm if only the person dreaming believes seriously in his dream, if he attentively observes life, compares his observations with his castles in the air... and works conscientiously for the achievement of his fantasies. If there is some connection between dreams and life then all is well.' To which Lenin added: 'Of this kind of dreaming there is unfortunately too little in our movement. And the people most responsible for this are those who boast of their sober views, their "closeness" to the "concrete"...'

We have already discussed how this connection between 'dreams and life' eluded the Russian Revolution, how 'this kind of dreaming' which was integral to Lenin's politics, lost out as the Revolution degenerated in the Soviet Union, and the dream soured, even became a nightmare. What needs to be noted in the immediate context is that 'this kind of dreaming', that Lenin deemed imperative, is today largely missing or stands abandoned in the mainstream Left politics, and this loss or abandonment of socialist vision is often rationalised or defended, much in the manner of what Lenin described as 'sober views' and '"closeness" to the "concrete"', in the name of 'realism'; as if realism necessarily permits only conservative, pragmatic or reformist, essentially non-visionary options in politics, which is simply not the case. It is certainly essential to be realistic. But a realistic understanding of the objective circumstances can as well demand radical, even revolutionary politics as has indeed become imperative today. As Marx himself put it long ago: 'These circumstances cry out: "Things cannot remain that way, they must become different and we ourselves, we human beings, must make them different"'. It is with as good reason that the rebel students of Paris had insisted in 1968: 'Be realist, attempt the impossible!' Today it seems as if the reactionary argument that you can't change human nature has triumphed after all, this time round in the guise of 'a hard-headed post-fundamentalist, post-utopian realism'. This conservative realism which starts from the way people are at any particular time and assumes that that is how they always will be, has to be categorically rejected. As Gramsci put it most succinctly: 'The question "What is man?" is really "What can man become?"' We must refuse to accept that what is, or has been, is all that can be, and insist that the human species has the ability to *develop* its capacities and to build a better world, that we can dream with sober senses.

It is indeed imperative that we refuse the temptation of cosy incorporation in the new rightist realism and assert an autonomous, historically situated revolutionary realism. Raymond Williams used to urge that socialists should not make long-term accommodation with short-term conditions. The challenge for the present generation indeed remains, as Williams once said, 'enough of us can reasonably believe that a new human order is seriously possible'. The future of socialism very much depends on socialists recovering their vision of this 'new human order', recovering in Bourdieu's words, 'a sense of utopian possibility', which, he says, 'it is one of neoliberalism's key victories to have killed off, or made to look antiquated.'

It is true that socialism is not about drawing blueprints of society of the future, about, as Marx said, building up 'the future in advance' and settling 'all problems for all times'. Not that Marx or socialists have nothing substantive to say on the subject. They have. And, while classical Marxism is quite legitimately relatively silent about it, with the Soviet experience behind them, socialists today have much more to say about what a socialist society should or should not be, or what should or should not be done in building a socialist society. Even so, for Marxism the responsibility for shaping this society lies only with those who are called upon to build it. And, it may be added, this building is not viewed in 'quasi-religious Salvationist' terms wherein socialism is supposed to cure all ills, solve all problems, finally lift all the burdens which have always plagued humankind, ensure complete cleansing of all that was evil in the world. On the contrary, the perspective that governs the building of socialism remains what it is for every stage in the struggle for socialism in which, to put it in the words of Ralph Miliband, socialism is viewed not 'as an achieved state' but rather as 'an objective involving permanent striving'. 'The struggle for freedom and justice', Chomsky has written, is 'unending', often 'grim', ever facing 'temptations or disillusionment... many failures and only limited successes', but 'never hopeless' – and it always goes on. This is also how the struggle for socialism, the building of a socialist society, needs to be viewed – an 'unending' struggle in the course of which as they change their world, human beings also change themselves.

None of this however obviates the need for a prior vision of the socialist future, the 'new human order' we seek. No sustained political struggle is possible without the hope of a better society that we can, in principle and in outline imagine. All emancipatory projects will come to nothing if the bulk of people become convinced that one cannot change, at best merely refurbish things, precisely what the bourgeois ideologues are today trying to convince them of. They denounce what cannot be realised within the established order as 'mere utopia' – as

Marcuse pointed out long ago – and are busy propagating the myth that utopian thought has been a prime force for violence in the modern age – ignoring the fact that more blood has been shed in our time by imperialist aggressions, bureaucratic miscalculation, racism, nationalism or religions sectarianism than through utopian dreams, to say nothing of 'the terrible costs of not changing the existing order', as Jawaharlal Nehru in one of his more lucid, Marxist moments once phrased it. The utopian impulse, human's vision of a better society, is in fact what has fuelled social progress throughout our history. 'Traum' Marx called it as he envisioned the future society beyond capitalism in which 'the free development each is the condition for the free development of all', 'the realm of freedom... beyond the sphere of actual material production (where) begins that development of human power which is an end in itself'. Such a vision of the future does not mean casting aside involvement with the present. On the contrary, providing a perspective for the ongoing and emerging struggles, it makes for a correct and more effective involvement with the present.

The robust Marxism of Karl Marx – unlike the flaccid Soviet Marxism which had, except in words, lost all sense of what socialism is about and bred reformism in the associated communist parties abroad – provides for such a vision, not as a utopian construction but through a critique of capitalism that establishes the basis for its negation in socialism: a critique of capitalist economy's absolute priority of profit-making and accumulation and the accompanying consumerist compulsions regardless of its consequences for humans and nature, to be negated by an economy which gives absolute priority to genuine human needs and is ecologically sustainable; a critique of capitalist politics as class domination and oppression and the exclusive business of a professionalised elite, to be negated by democracy as a process that permeates every structure of society and overcomes the separation between the governed and the governors; a critique of capitalist alienation and dehumanisation, to be negated by a non-alienated, truly rich life beyond the realm of actual material production, with the human beings appropriating the world with all their glorious *human* senses. It is this Marxist critique of capitalist reality that goes into the making of the Marxist vision of socialism/communism – the vision of a remade world, a truly free, ethically and aesthetically satisfying world, one that capitalism both rejects and makes impossible.

Obviously, this vision is possible of realisation only with the replacement of capitalism as a social formation that places priority on profits and markets. But the Marxist critique also involves the conclusion that this can only be achieved through the conscious action and practice of those who in one way or another are its victims and come to 'win the theoretical awareness of (their) loss' as Marx put it. Despite the reversals of the recent past, this awareness, in however rudimentary a form, is already there and will only grow with the passage of time. The material deprivations and damage of global capitalism are only too evident in the world as whole, and the sensitive people everywhere are recognising and protesting its moral and cultural consequences, even if it will be some time before the interconnections are seen more fully and clearly. There is a growing expression of a need for things that cannot be measured in terms of money or judged only by the criteria of the market place, as also a need for direct human contact and communication. There are demands for liberation of labour from being a commodity and from work that alienates us from ourselves, for returning to labour its creativity and giving autonomy to our life-style. In fact if we look deep enough into contemporary society we will see that given its economic political and moral-cultural crisis, it is far richer in oppositional moods and potential than is generally acknowledged; old and new contradictions are producing an unwritten anti-capitalist critique of their own, thereby reinforcing recognition of the need for socialism not as an ideological construct but as the result of experience itself. What is required is to help people see the interconnections more fully and clearly so that they move into action against capitalism.

'Proletarian revolutions', Marx had written, 'deride with unmerciful thoroughness the inadequacies, weaknesses and paltriness of their first attempts'. But, as a revolutionary, Marx had also brought us, socialists, the gift of historical optimism. Therefore even as they come to terms with 'the inadequacies, weaknesses and paltriness', indeed the failure of the 'attempt' in the Soviet Union, it is imperative for socialists to revive and renew their historic legacy, to recover and uphold the socialist vision of a new human order. They need to be confident in their fundamental beliefs and values and firmly counter the free-market celebrations, which are in any case already on the wane. In other words, they must not be afraid to be socialist. Instead they must openly and frankly assert that a better future for humanity is impossible under capitalism, that socialism remains the only realistic and realisable alternative to capitalism, an epochal alternative that is not just a more progressive version of the industrial capitalist system based on state-controlled development of the same productive forces, but a new way of life, based on use-value and democratic planning, renewable energies and ecological care, race and gender equality, fraternity and international solidarity – indeed a new civilisation in which, as Bertrand Russell once put it, 'the creative spirit is alive, in which life is an adventure full of hope and joy, based rather upon the impulse to construct than upon the desire to retain what we possess or to seize what is possessed by others'.

The commitment to and hope for a society thus based on humanist values indeed requires a utopian vision. But, again, this society must not be conceived as a paradise regained, a blue-print realised or a model achieved, or as a 'once for all' affair, a 'final' state of society. Engels had written: 'Just as knowledge is unable to reach a perfect termination in a perfect, ideal condition of humanity, so is history unable to do so; a perfect society, a perfect "state", are things which can only exist in imagination... (the) dialectical philosophy dissolves all conceptions of final, absolute truth, and of a final, absolute state of humanity corresponding to it. For it nothing is final, absolute, sacred'. Thus, no more than capitalism can such a society of socialist vision be 'the end of history'. For Marx, 'Communism' was no end-state of any sort that vulgarisers have made it out to be, but the beginning, at last, of a truly *human* history of mankind.

It is thus that a utopian vision needs to be recovered and sustained and the Promethean spirit underlying socialism as an emanicipatory project preserved. Against the tremendous counter-revolutionary offensive that stresses the eternity of capitalism, socialists must continue to proclaim the permanence of revolution and represent what Ernst Bloch called the 'Principle of Hope', the utopia of an emancipated society.

XI

Socialists' loss of their vision of the future has, as we have seen, many negative consequences for their politics. The most important such consequence, to be specifically noted, is that socialists seem to have lost the capacity to think in terms of a different, alternative project in opposition to the currently dominant capitalist project. People are being driven by their conditions to protest and rebel, movements with distinct anti-systemic thrust are coming up everywhere. The absence of a socialist vision of the future and, therefore, of a radical alternative geared to it, cripples and frustrates these emerging struggles of the people, even helps the enemy to divert popular discontent and frustration in dangerous directions. Again, it is idle to expect people to engage in sustained political action for an alternative social order unless they know something about the ends and the means, about where we are going and how we intend to get there. After the broken hopes and shattered dreams of the recent past, it is all the more clear that no movement will now embark on a long, historical journey without knowing what it is aiming at and what is the route to it. Socialists therefore need to recover the capacity to think and act in terms of an alternative socialist project. That this project has to be formulated for each different country is obvious enough – the nation-state remains the main arena of struggle for socialism. Obviously, the strategy and tactics will vary from country to country and the struggle in each country has to find its own answers to its problems. But while such diversity is both necessary and desirable there is still one overriding consideration. The current success of capitalism rendering reformist gradualism irrelevant and its adherents themselves abandoning their socialism altogether, revolutionary socialism is the sole realistic agenda today. More than ever before, a socialist project today has to be a project of revolutionary socialism and its politics, diversity notwithstanding, has to be revolutionary politics. But here at least one clarification is in order.

Revolutionary politics does not mean thinking and acting in terms of storming the Bastille or seizing the Winter Palace, or launching an immediate armed struggle. There are socialists for whom revolutionary politics is unthinkable except in association with a revolutionary upheaval. For them the task is to set about organising this upheaval, 'to make a revolution' – anything else is dangerous and discredited reformism. This is a wholly mistaken view in that it misses out on the necessarily long period of preparatory ideological and political struggles that go into the making of a socialist revolution, even if it is viewed as an upheaval. At its worst this view even ends up as so much posturing, an alibi for doing nothing. This is not to deny or foreclose the issue that situations may be there in some parts of the world where the main task is to concentrate on organising a revolution, though even here success is most likely only if the task is undertaken with due care and preparation, which does not necessarily rule out all 'reformist' activity. But the situation generally, and certainly in most parts of the world today, is one of long haul. The main task here is to reach out to the people, organise their class and mass struggles, constantly raise these struggles to the level of political struggles, and relate them to the overall objective of revolutionary transformation of society, the socialist revolution we seek. It is only through such struggles that people will learn to need and make this revolution, whatever eventual shape or form it takes.

This is not an easy task to carry out. Here we are indeed face to face with a problem that is as old as socialism itself. The movement for socialism has an inevitable duality within it. A socialist movement has to fight within the framework of existing capitalist society but must inevitably offer solutions which ultimately lie beyond that framework; it has to struggle for a socialist future from within a capitalist present. If it concentrates too much on that future it runs the risk of sectarian isolation. Yet if it limits itself to struggle within the system, it loses its original *raison d'etre*, the search for a radically different society. The task for the socialist movement thus is to preserve a permanent link between its current partial or defensive struggles and its vision of a future socialist society which is at once distant and crucial. As the *Communist Manifesto* has it: 'The Communists fight for the attainment of the immediate aims, for the enforcement of the momentary interests of the working class; but in the movement of the present, they also represent and take care of the future of that movement'. At the tactical level we have the Leninist insistence that socialists must constantly relate specific grievances to a criticism of the system *as a whole*, constantly showing how they are linked together and therefore how people's specific struggles are also linked to the struggle for a revolutionary transformation of society. In other words, the key task is to establish linkages between theory and practice which would lead everyday resistance beyond short-term demands towards socialism. As Lenin, among many others including Gramsci, understood, these linkages did not spontaneously emerge from ordinary working class life or struggle. It was up to socialists to perceive them theoretically and then forge them into practices or actions which made sense to the working people and linked their ongoing struggles to the coming of a socialist future.

Though easy to formulate in theory, what is involved here is possibly the most difficult yet vital practical task in the struggle for socialism: to link the *immediate* (necessarily reformist) activity with the *ultimate* (essentially revolutionary) objectives; or to phrase it differently, to preserve the integrity of the *ultimate* perspective without losing contact with the *immediate* demands, determinations and potentialities of the historically given conditions. Struggle for the immediate or limited aims and objectives is how people, necessarily, begin their struggle against the system and for a better life. Important as a way of saying *'NO'* to capitalism in a concrete manner or winning gains for the people, given *socialist* leadership, this struggle can also be a means of enhancing people's consciousness and organisation for the ultimate socialist transformation. Reform and revolution thus must not be seen as mutually exclusive opposites. The task rather is to subordinate reform to revolution.

This is how Marx had argued in his controversy with Bakunin and anarchists. As a revolutionary, Marx rejected voluntarism. As against his opponents who tended to rely on 'spontaneity' and 'instinctive conscience of the popular masses', Marx viewed the development of a *socialist mass consciousness* as necessary for a socialist revolution and revolutionary reconstruction of society. For him this was possible only through struggles over a long period.

To conclude, even as we recognise that struggle for socialism, as always, is a *revolutionary* struggle and that socialist politics is nothing if it is not *revolutionary* politics, it does not mean any kind of rejection of reforms. What is demanded is that socialists struggle for reforms as revolutionaries, that is, they remain faithful to socialist principles, imbue the necessarily partial popular struggles with socialist consciousness, put *socialist meaning* into people's experience as they struggle for, win or lose, reforms, and thus help them become more effective subjects or makers of the socialist revolution, in whatever shape or form it has to be eventually made.

XII

Providing revolutionary leadership to partial, reformist struggles is only a part of the more basic task that faces the socialists today. The struggle for socialism, or a more or less prolonged transition to socialism, will of course be governed by the historical specificities of the situation in different countries of the world. But everywhere it involves the question of hegemony in society, a renewed ideological-political struggle to so build up a movement for socialism that it wins a cultural-intellectual hegemony, becomes increasingly the enlightened common-sense of our age. Such hegemonising is always hard work but it has become particularly hard now with the Soviet collapse and the resumed global domination of capitalism.

Ruling classes, controlling society's economic surplus have also always exercised control over ideological-cultural activity, generating ideas, ideologies and culture to justify and preserve their social order. Extended use of 'Ideological State Apparatuses' as Althusser called them, to secure hegemony over society has been an important capitalist state activity, a part of one of its principal functions, namely, to ensure the defence and reproduction of capitalist social relations. The failure of Soviet socialism has naturally made for strengthened bourgeois hegemony over society, a more widespread acceptance of bourgeois ideology among the people. In the few years since the Soviet collapse, a great deal of socialist inheritance has been eclipsed and in the developing darkness much necessarily lost sight of. The very idea of socialism has been delegitimised, and there is widespread acceptance of TINA – 'there is no alternative' to capitalism. In the neoliberal offensive that is on, increasingly, it is media and entertainment industry which are setting the ideological-cultural agenda for society with a special focus on commercialisation of youth culture. New variants of bourgeois ideology (including post-modernism) have come up overwhelming every dissident point of view and converging in 'a cynical defeatism, where every radical programme of change is doomed to failure'.

In this situation the necessity of ideological struggle for socialism, the search for hegemony in social and political life is obvious. Without developing the ideological-cultural forces to challenge the media fostered consensus over the inevitability of capitalism, without developing and fostering the capacity to think in ways independent of capitalist ideas, building a movement for socialism would be inconceivable. As has been well said: 'You can't fight an enemy that has outposts in your head'. A struggle for such hegemony in society was indeed always entailed in classical Marxism, by its concept of ideology and the recognition that 'ruling ideas', which are always 'the ideas of the ruling class', need to be countered and overcome by the working class in pursuit of its emancipation. The struggle has now to be waged with renewed vigour with the help of insights provided by later Marxists from Lenin to Althusser, particularly Gramsci with his insistence that the revolutionary movement must seek to acquire 'civil hegemony' as a necessary prerequisite of effective acquisition and exercise of political power.

In this renewed struggle for hegemony the principal task of socialists and communists immediately is to try to restore the credibility of socialism in the consciousness of the common people. This means not only ridding the concept of 'socialism' of the taint that Soviet deformations have imparted it, but bringing masses of men and women to the conviction of the necessity and feasibility of building socialism – a socialism which, taking into account the past experience and new awareness of recent decades, will be a truly democratic and egalitarian society, cooperative and self-governing at different levels, politically and otherwise pluralist, free from gender, race or caste oppressions, environment-friendly, and radically pacifist and internationalist; its economy based on a genuine social ownership that dissolving the existing structures of power and privilege, transfers economic power from private hands into public domain, and functioning according to democratic economic planning with people empowered to choose between different variants of the economic plan and impose correction when necessary. It will be a society on the road to 'the realm of freedom beyond the sphere of actual material production', as visualised by Marx.

We recreate people's faith in the necessity and feasibility of socialism not by preaching it but through a genuinely critical assessment of the Soviet experience and, above all, through a critique of capitalism that touches on both its most modern and dynamic aspects and their negative consequences, now visible as never before, and the emancipatory change it concretely points to. The negative consequences are manifest not only in capitalism's now intensified exploitation of the people everywhere, but also in the growth of ethnic, nationalist and religious conflicts that are a marked feature of the post-Soviet collapse world of global capitalism under the U.S. domination. We have to help people understand that here, again, the solution lies in what socialists are arguing for. As Ralph Miliband said in one of his last lectures: 'In the long term, the hope that ethnic and national racism might be effectively subdued and turned into no more than a minor nuisance, must rest on the coming into being of societies in which men and women would be assured of a secure material existence, with the guarantee of essential civic and political freedoms, where cooperation and friendship would be genuine rather than rhetorical principles of social organisation. Communist regimes failed to create these conditions; and so, in different ways is capitalism unable to create them... A radically different social order seems nowadays remote; but the notion that such an alternative belongs to the realm of fantasy, and that there is no point in striving for it, is a gratuitous surrender to the many voices which preach the conservative message that there is no alternative to the here and now'...

In the struggle for hegemony, the 'counter-hegemonic struggle' as Miliband called it, alongside a wide range of activities to develop a democratic socialist culture among the people to sustain them in their daily living and struggle for a better life, an independent socialist educational movement needs to be built up, separate from the mainstream of schools, colleges and universities which by and large purvey one or other forms of dominant bourgeois ideology. This is a permanent requirement. There is no shortage of materials for imparting this education. Today we know far more about the workings of capitalism, in the metropolitan centres as well as third world countries, than ever before in the history of bourgeois civilisation. What is lacking are organised efforts and facilities – tutors, classes, study circles, etc. – to take this knowledge to the people, to provide for regular discussion and interaction, debate and argument, using all the theoretical resources of the socialist heritage but with no one bringing down the Tablets from on high or indulging in 'heresy-hunting' polemics. This political educational work is particularly important in the mass organisations of the workers, peasants and other sections of the working people which will help them understand their place in the world at large and what they need to do about it. With the theoretical wreckage left behind by 'official Marxism', even 'preaching to the converted' is not to be derided. Many of 'the converted' can surely do with lots of 'preaching' today, lots of re-education in what it is all about.

Ralph Miliband has written:

> Words like 'political education' and 'political training' are nowadays highly suspect on the Left, not surprisingly since they evoke the kind of frozen catechisms that long passed for socialist education in Communist and other Marxist organisations; and so too, from a different perspective, do the words attract suspicion and hostility because they are thought to have an 'elitist' ring, and are taken to convey the notion of experts passing on their wisdom and knowledge to the ignorant hewers of wood and drawers of water.
>
> Yet, socialist education need not have these connotations, and can be a true process of cooperative learning, in which the questioning of everything is not only accepted but understood to be essential to that process. This also answers the accusation of 'elitism'; for what is or should be involved in socialist education, properly understood, is not a one-way process of communication but on the contrary a dialogue in which teachers and taught enlighten and stimulate each other in a constant exchange of ideas.
>
> At any rate, socialist education is a crucial component part of counter-hegemonic struggles, and requires organised and systematic, institutionalised forms as well as other, individual and independent forums. This requirement is something which earlier socialist generations took for granted, and did meet, well or ill is not here the point. Stalinist experience, in this realm as in all others, provides a salutary lesson in what ought not to be done. But the need remains for 'schools of socialism', open, flexible, critical and disputatious, and able to send out into the world activists better equipped to counter the propaganda which helps dominant classes to maintain themselves in power, and to present a persuasive case of socialism.
>
> It is of course true that these ideological struggles are only one part of a much wider class struggle; but they are an important part of it. For they help to inform and shape the language, the spirit and the aims of class struggle, and give it a greater resilience than it would otherwise possess. The present may seem a bad time for counter-ideological strivings. But the collapse of Communist regimes, and the ever-greater adaptation of social democracy to capitalism, in fact offer a new space and new

> opportunities for such strivings, and make the coming years a period of hope rather than despair.

The current subalternism of the post-colonial ruling elites in the third world, their accommodation or surrender to 'globalisation' makes for a similar conclusion.

This 'counter-hegemonic' educational movement certainly needs to use the theoretical and moral resources of *all* the revolutionary or emancipatory traditions of the country as also to learn from the experience of radical or popular movements which have focussed on the formation of radical social consciousness (such as, for example, Makarenko's work with war orphans in the Ukraine in the 1920s, the feminist consciousness raising groups,Paulo Freire's concientizaciao, liberation theology's base communities, participatory action research, etc.). But Marxism remains central to any effort towards formation of socialist consciousness and equipping people with revolutionary theory. True, Marxism, as a wholly new body of ideas for understanding and changing the world grew out of the proletarian experience in the West, expressive, above all, of the revolutionary interests of the proletariat; and it remained very much a Western-centred movement in the period between Marx's death and the Russian Revolution, a fact which reflected the economic and even more the political realities of the time. But, as we have argued earlier, Marx and Engels were not proletarians, and having once come into being, Marxism is in no sense the exclusive property of the proletariat or a western phenomenon. Like science and knowledge generally, it is a part of the heritage of humankind, and certainly available for appropriation by the working people intheir emanicipatory struggles anywhere in the world.

It may be pointed out that Marx, throughout his life, attached the greatest importance to socialist education of the working class. This is evident in the way he wrote and viewed his writings – giving of his 'best' to the working people – in the intense pedagogical efforts that went into the organisation of the First International, in his travels to workers' educational conferences and the long tedious hours spent explaining things to them, in his life-long ideological struggles devoted to clarifying theoretical and practical issues of the workers' movement, and so on. Marx rejected politics based on 'exhortation'. It has to be based on knowledge, on a proper understanding of things. For him, as a contemporary, Paul Annenkov, has repored: 'to ruse the population without giving them any firm well thought-out reasons for their activity would be simply to deceive them.' 'Ignorance', Marx insisted, 'never yet helped anybody'. As he saw it, transformation of the working class from 'a class in itself' to 'a class for itself', transformation of the oppressed people into a force for socialist revolution, requires along with political organisation, transformed social consciousness. And this is where socialist education or the spread of socialist ideology has an important role to play.

The emphasis on political education or ideological work does not mean that those committed to socialism remain content with postulating socialism as a strategic objective and defining and propagating its identity at the level of ideas. The conviction that there are profound objective reasons for the reconstruction of a worldwide anti-capitalist movement does not exhaust itself in theorising in terms of *la longue duree* or epochal transitions. It is necessary to link down this strategic objective and theorising with political practice in a determinate short-term future and acquire leverage over immediate contradictions and forces that are at work in society. Capitalism is an inherently contradictory and unstable social order. It continues to have its own deepening crises when, as *Communist Manifesto* put it, 'man is at last compelled to face with sober senses his real conditions of life and his relations with his kind', and, therefore, also compelled to rebel. It is the task of socialists to provide plausible and practical understanding so that people find progressive ways to rebel. Without such help, there is a strong chance that rebels will not be able to say *NO* to capitalism effectively. Socialist education or theorising, thus linked with their practical activity helps people to see through the structural power of capitalism to obscure social relations and recognise what capitalism really is, and also suggests how it can be best fought and transformed. Socialism assumes people's capacity to transform their world and this entails popular understanding of and participation in this transformation. Socialist education or ideological work is the bridge, carrying traffic both ways between the practice of theory and the practice of revolution.

This traffic between theory and practice is a precondition for any programme of effective socialist politics. The essence of revolutionary socialist politics lies precisely in establishing this theory-based linkage between the ultimate and the immediate in the ongoing popular struggles. The failure to do so, one-sided emphasis on one or the other inevitably leads to either revolutionary adventurism or economistic reformism. In fact the ideal of socialism itself can regain its credibility in the consciousness of people only if it thus becomes relevant to the needs and concerns of the people, to their everyday struggles. (It may be added that radical theory, if bereft of practical political context, tends to fray at the edges and sag in the middle, to be, in Perry Anderson's words, 'inevitably deformed or eclipsed', as has not unoften happened with Marxism itself.)

What is at issue in our argument here is the question of developing a revolutionary consciousness among the working people. Socialist education certainly has its importance in creating and fostering it. But it is necessary to recognise that people's consciousness is formed during the daily experience of living and the interpretation of that experience on the basis of their knowledge and previous experience. It does not change simply by urging it to change, by exhortation and offer of better arguments, or even by teaching systematically another, socialist world view – however important all this may be. It requires an altered practice as well as a *socialist* interpretation of every old and new practice, so that daily experience supports the socialist view or outlook; and this is true as much of the period of the revolutionary struggle for power as of the post-revolutionary period of socialist construction. Hence the centrality of practical activity, of *socialist* political practice in the struggle for hegemony in society.

As already noticed, Marx always recognised, for himself and for others, the educating and liberating quality of revolutionary practice, the purifying power of revolutionary activity in transforming the very nature of those involved in it. Using the metaphor of 'civil war' for class struggle, he wrote: 'we say to the workers: you have 15, 20, 50 years of civil war to go through in order to alter the situation and to train yourself for the exercise of power.' Again, apropos the Paris Commune: 'the working class did not expect miracles from the Commune. They have no ready-made utopias to introduce *par decret du peuple*. They know that in order to work out their own emancipation, and along with it that higher form to which present society is irresistibly tending through its own economic development, they will have to pass through long struggles, through a series of historical processes, in the course of which men, no less than circumstances, will be completely transformed.'

Sam Gindin has written: 'For the ruling class, the idea of ruling is "in their bones", assumed by osmosis from everything around them – from the nervous care of a series of nannies, to the games they play as children, the walls that surround their homes and gardens, the trees that shade their houses, their generational expectations, and, of course, their privileged access to resources of every kind. The ruling class literally breathes power. But for workers, the idea of "ruling" is an absence. It is not even a distant goal facing possibly insurmountable problems; it hasn't, generally, yet manifested itself as an *idea* to be confronted. For reasons rooted in the working class family and the workplace, and well cultivated beyond, the tendency of capitalism is to reduce a working class with the potential capacities to do, enjoy, and act politically, to a collection of "just workers"; "just consumers"; and "just voters". In contrast to the ruling class, workers know their place even as they resent it and must go through a process of *unlearning* before the idea of collectively running their lives, and not just occasionally influencing them, can be born.' At the heart of this process of 'unlearning,' and learning to win and exercise power, lies 'revolutionising practice' as Marx called it. People's power to emancipate themselves, to construct and run an emancipated society, grows out of their practical activity, their own struggles and the revolutionary consciousness they are suffused with.

Socialists, for that matter working people themselves, have primarily two basic weapons or resources in their struggle: organisation and consciousness, the latter, viewed broadly, inclusive of dimensions of science and ethics, of knowledge and a moral commitment – to 'work for humanity' is how Marx phrased it early in his life. The place of organisation in revolutionary struggle is generally accepted, but it is the question of revolutionary consciousness which has today emerged as a matter of decisive importance, in pre-revolutionary struggle as much as in post-revolutionary socialist construction. 'The task of the revolutionary is to make revolution', said Che Guevara. But this always implied the key task of changing consciousness and acquiring revolutionary theory, without which no revolution can be made or any socialism built. Certainly the material and moral circumstances created by capitalism can produce a critical social awareness and even direct our attention to the solutions which socialism proposes, but this does not by itself create socialist consciousness, which taking many forms and drawing from different sources, yet needs to be actively fostered and advanced.

This fostering and advancement certainly includes educational-cultural efforts to bring socialist ideology, especially Marxist theory, to the people. But such efforts must not be viewed in authoritarian and paternalistic, or substitutionist terms, a matter of people needing to 'be educated' from above, something that Marx categorically rejected in his *Theses on Feuerbach* and elsewhere. Such efforts need to be organically linked to the process of people learning through their experience or struggles, their self-education as opposed to instruction handed down. As Rosa Luxemburg well emphasised: 'the proletariat requires a high degree of political education, of class consciousness and organization. All these conditions cannot be fulfilled by pamphlets and leaflets, but only by the living political school, in the continuous course of the revolution.' The workers, she had insisted, learn best 'in the school of action'. This is how Che Guevara put it, as Cuba set on the road to socialism: 'The first step to educate the people is to introduce them to the revolution. Never pretend you can help them conquer their rights by education alone, while they must endure a despotic government. First and foremost, teach them to conquer their rights and, as they gain representation in the government, they will learn whatever they are taught and much more: with no great effort they shall soon become the teachers, towering above the rest.' Socialist pedagogy that fosters and advances socialist consciousness must be viewed as enabling people to educate themselves through revolutionary practice or, as Marx put it in the *German Ideology*, 'in revolutionary activity, personal change coincides with a modification of conditions'.

The struggle for hegemony in society is hard work but absolutely indispensable. Intellectual-political struggle to establish the credibility of socialism as a necessary and feasible project, to foster socialist consciousness among the people, imperative at all times, is all the more necessary in view of the paradoxical situation obtaining in the world today. On the one hand there is capitalism, globally dominant as never before, but regularly failing to deliver on its promises. Its record over the past decade is, to say the least, most dismal. What is on offer by either neo-liberalism or social democracy, or their third world variants, provides no solutions to world's manifold problems. The waste and inagalitarianism of capitalism's 'unregulated' market is evident throughout the world. The majority of people, more so in the third world, are experiencing deteriorating living standards, growing social and personal insecurity, and decay in public services, while affluent minorities continue to prosper as never before. The third world is indeed being further peripheralised. On the other hand, while people are resisting and fighting back, this is largely confined to sporadic revolts, local struggles, large-scale protests of short duration, mostly 'economist' in nature. Popular resistance is growing and it certainly has its potential for the resumed struggle for socialism, but so far it is not socialist, and except in rare cases, even not yet fundamentally anti-capitalist. There are no significant political projects which articulate and campaign for a socialist alternative to capitalism. In other words, what we have in the world today is a profound gap between the worsening conditions of life of the people on the one hand and the weakness of revolutionary or radical response to it on the other. The objective situation of growing inequalities and socio-economic regression is not accompanied by the growth of subjective forces capable of transforming this situation. Hence the paramount need of a struggle for hegemony, for a wide-ranging intellectual-cultural intervention (in the areas of ideology, education, consciousness, practical action, etc.) that transforms the subjective response, the growing popular resistance into a sustained struggle for a socialist alternative to capitalism.

XIII

Classical Marxism visualised the struggle for socialism as a class struggle; Marx indeed saw 'revolution' as 'the highest form of class struggle'. Socialism was not just a changing of capitalism, but a revolutionary reconstruction of society on an entirely altered class basis of economy and politics, leading ultimately to a classless society. In a fundamental sense, this still remains the case. Not to be interpreted in narrow economistic or reductionist terms 'class' and 'class struggle' remain central not only to Marxist analysis of society but also to the struggle for socialism. The economic, political and ideological 'barrier fortresses' of ruling class power cannot be demolished except through principled and consistent class struggle. Recent developments, including the collapse in the Soviet Union, do not change this; only a few explanatory or clarificatory observations and renewed emphasis is called for.

The concept of class has been the subject of endless debate over the years. Along with the notion implicit in the above quote, Marx, in tune with the vocabulary and verbal conventions of his time, was not averse to using the term 'class' in the loose popular sense. Thus we find him writing, with or without quotation marks, of 'ideological etc. classes', the 'unproductive classes', the 'serving [or servant] class', the 'educated classes', the class of 'professional conspirators', the 'servile class of lawyers', artificial 'classes' fabricated in British India, or the confrontation between 'two particular classes of capitalists' (moneyed and industrial), and so on. The dynamics of class-like formations outside the boundaries of stable situations, of classes in the process of being born or becoming, dying out or decaying into something else, only complicates the problem. There have been all sorts of helpful, not helpful and plain misleading definitions. Even the helpful ones, for example Lenin's – according to Lenin, 'Classes are large groups of people differing from each other by the place they occupy in a historically determined system of social production, by their relation (in most cases fixed and formulated by law) to the means of production, by their role in the social organisation of labour, and, consequently, by the dimensions of the share of social wealth of which they dispose and the mode of acquiring it. Classes are groups of people one of which can appropriate the labour of another owing to the different places they occupy in a definite system of social economy' – have their weaknesses as indeed all brief definitions or characterisations must have.

Since Marx himself has been regularly reproached by Marxologists for failing to provide a definition of 'class' which they can recognise as such, even though he made important use of the concept throughout his work, it will perhaps not be out of place to digress a little on the subject of 'definition' itself.

Conventional academic scholarship has always had a certain fascination for 'definition'. May be for reasons of pedagogy and the examinations that go with it. It could also be that the empiricistic mode naturally tends to abridge or congeal social reality into a lexicographic formula, a definition. But given Marxism's dialectical mode of thinking, 'definition' is, if not alien, certainly not that important in Marxian method of social analysis. Marx had argued that to abstract a social or economic phenomenon, for example, 'property', from its 'specific relationships' and then define it as if it were 'an independent relation, a category apart, an abstract and eternal idea can be nothing but an illusion of metaphysics or jurisprudence'. Engels had warned against looking for 'fixed and universally applicable definitions' in Marx's work. He had, on his part, insisted that defining or conceptualisation must not involve a freezing of social phenomenon into a static formula. He wrote: 'It is a matter of course that, where things and their mutual interrelations are conceived not as fixed but as changing, their mental images, the ideas concerning them are likewise subject to change and transformation; that they cannot be sealed up in rigid definitions, but must be developed in the historical and logical process of their formation.'

Thus, in an important sense, all definitions are deficient or inadequate and from a strictly scientific standpoint of rather limited value. A definition takes on a concrete meaning only when flushed or filled up with the specific social relations that constitute the reality of a phenomenon in a given social order. This however is not to deny that, subject to the above-mentioned considerations, definitions can be convenient or useful, at times even indispensable, as the way to begin, as a guide to social analysis. A good definition will of course point to the most common, the simplest or essential in a phenomenon. But it should also be suggestive of the complex socio-historical relationships that go into the making of its concrete reality as a part of the social whole – thereby providing a point of entry into a study of this social whole as well, with its underlying structural necessities or determinations.

That Marx never gave a formal definition of class, and it continues to be described as an 'ambiguous', even 'mysterious' identity, does not mean that we are clueless about what is essentially involved here. As we have noticed earlier, Marxism views society as a social whole, or 'totality', a historically specific structured interdependence of parts, which is loaded with the predominance in the long run of one part within it, the economy (or more precisely 'the mode of production' with its 'relations of production' or the economic structural base) and with contradictions that account for its dynamics, its concrete over-determined historical development. In this view, born essentially of Marx's analysis of capitalism but with larger relevance, the structural importance of the economy lies in the fact that, as Marx put it, it is 'the direct relationship of the owners of the conditions of production to the direct producers... which holds the inner-most secret, the hidden foundation of the entire social structure.' This relationship, a relationship of exploitation between the class of direct producers and the class that controls the appropriation of the surplus product of their labour, around which the rest of the class structure takes shape, including elements left over from obsolete social forms, forms the skeleton around which a given mode of production is socially structured. It is the dominant form of 'surplus appropriation', through exploitation of others' labour, which gives its character to economy and therefore to a particular society. A part of this basic understanding, class, as a fundamental concept in Marx's theory, denotes a relationship of exploitation. It is the collective social expression of the fact of exploitation which in pointing to the way in which exploitation is structurally embedded in a social formation also underlines the centrality of class as a structural component of a given society.

Pointing out that 'class dynamics is the foundation of all of Marx's politics... the "transmission belt" between his social-historical and political theory; or, to change the image, it constitutes the latter's drive shaft', Hal Draper has thus explained Marx's concept of class:

> In popular usage, a class is merely any group of people sharing some common characteristic(s). A 'social class' may be seen as sharing certain social characteristics – say, rank; an 'economic class' may be deduced from income brackets; and so on. These are *classifications*, the result of classifying people according to some more or less relevant criterion. For many loose-jointed purposes there need be no reasonable objection to such a usage. Contrary to a widespread misapprehension, Marx himself not infrequently used class in similar loose or broad ways when convenient. The issue is not whether this common use is wrong in itself, but rather what it is used for, what it is considered relevant to.
>
> This popular usage implicitly regards a class attribute as a *manifestation* of society's structure, a derivative of it. But what if there are classes of people who share the common characteristic of forming a *structural element* of the society itself? Such a structural class is certainly more basic. In any case, in the context of Marx's theory a socio-economic class is a class of people playing a common role as a structural component of a given society.
>
> How this is concretized flows from Marx's theory itself. Historically, in Marx's view, class differentiation begins only with

> the appearance – due to development of the forces of production – of a *surplus product*; that is, that which is produced over and above the reproduction needs of the direct producer. This is the key to the meaning of class in Marx. Classes define themselves not simply in terms of the process of production (which existed before the separation into classes and will exist after classes are done away with); they must be defined in relation to *surplus* production, and specifically in relation to *control over the appropriation of the surplus product*.

Hal Drapper's formal definition of class, in the context of Marx's method of socio-historical analysis, is merely an 'algebraic' formula which takes on concrete meaning when it is fleshed out with the specific relationships of a specific social order, in the present case of specific social orders within global capitalism, at its centre and periphery or semi-periphery, existing at different levels of economic development, or transiting, and therefore making for a complex roster or configuration of classes underlying their social and political dynamics. I will only add that focus on 'surplus appropriation', viewing class as a relationship of exploitation, also provides us our concept of class struggle. The essence of class struggle is exploitation or resistance to it; there need not necessarily be any class consciousness or, for that matter, any political element in it. The class struggle that Marx *advocates* is the struggle waged by the victims of exploitation, class consciously, for their own ends, that is as a struggle for socialism.

To continue with the question of class and class struggle, *the* point of our argument is not what is generally conceded: that 'class remains the single most powerful determinant of life chances', or that 'the existence of vast concentrations of unelected and unaccountable power behind the facade of representative democracy, in the state bureaucracy and the military and security apparatuses, and in the multinational corporations and the financial markets' makes it 'hard to see how any strategy which seeks to address these realities can avoid the class divisions from which they are inseparable', or that 'during the past twelve years in the United States, and more or less elsewhere throughout the world, there have been growing class divisions between rich and poor, haves and have-nots' and that 'to proclaim the obsolescence of social classes and class struggle is absolutely wrong in the face of the unpalatable reality of class', etc. etc. All this is very true, pointing as it does to the obviously noticeable reality of class and class exploitation as an aspect of capitalism everywhere. The point however is that class is not just an aspect of capitalism among other aspects, it is *constitutive* of capitalism, which explains, on the one hand, the power of Marxist class analysis to understand and interpret social, political and cultural processes of capitalism – something that mainstream sociological instruments of analysis, such as 'status', or 'life style', or 'elite' etc., lacking the organic or structural relationship with society that is the hallmark of 'class', comparatively fail to do – and, on the other hand, the centrality of class-structural change for any radical transformation of society, which is the issue that class struggle foregrounds.

The economy or class-structural basis of capitalism, in an asymmetry of reciprocal influence, *decisively conditions* every other part or aspect of society, its politics, morality, culture, indeed the dynamics of its life as a whole. If capitalism in its hegemonic expansion leaves no dimension of life untouched – work and play, art and culture, family and community, war and governance, city and country – it is this integrative core which puts the distinctive stamp of the system on everything. It needs to be particularly noted that this everything excludes neither the already existing iniquities that capitalism inherits, nor the non-class oppressions which have an autonomous reality of their own – iniquities and oppressions relating to gender or patriarchy, race, war, caste, tribe, nationality or minorities, and so on. Even as capitalism preserves them, it alters their context and transforms their meaning. It absorbs them, as it were, into its own system of power and, in so doing often intensifies their severity. Marxist class analysis is about the integrative core of the system and about the interconnections between this core and other parts of the system inclusive of relations among the parts themselves. It deals with the *totality* of oppressions in society, but it sees the various forms of oppression as interrelated and mutually reinforcing within a common system of power and exploitation itself based on class, that indeed defines capitalism itself as 'class struggle', (however unpopular a reference to this reality or truth may be in this post-Soviet collapse, 'post-modern' era). That is why even as socialism as a common project of the people focuses on the abolition of class exploitation under capitalism, this remains a necessary, though by no means sufficient condition for the abolition of non-class oppressions; and why the struggle against these oppressions can be effective only by engaging in class-based people's polities. It must become a part of class struggle for socialism.

I shall have more to say on this subject in a later section. Immediately I would only like to point out that the above argument does not involve any economic or class reductionism. There is no denying the reality of multiple other than class social sites or subjectivities in society, or the importance and autonomy of the 'new social movements' based on identities other than class or motivated by other than class interests, or for that matter the fact that there are power struggles outside of the class bounds – where the notion of 'elites' may be a useful supplement to Marxist class analysis – or that both socialist and capitalist politics often represent an autonomous development beyond given class interests, however central or necessary the realisation of these interests may be to their purposes. It is only suggested that class is not just another 'site' or identity, it is a structural constituent of the social formation, that class relations, as it were, 'saturate' all other social relations, that their dynamic conditions the dynamics of non-class identities (including their struggles), and that without a change of its structural, that is, class basis, no fundamental change in society can be visualised. In other, more specific words, what is suggested is that, given the limits imposed by the structural or class logic of the system, the 'new social movements', even the best of 'identity' or 'special interest' struggles, will not go far within capitalism and no matter how far they go, the 'victories' they register, capitalism will continue to be the system it is today, a conflict-ridden, essentially authoritarian and brutalising social system, poisoned by its inability to make rational or humane use of the immense resources it has itself brought into being.

As mentioned in the beginning, 'class' and 'class struggle' remain central to our understanding of society and the struggle for socialism. It is particularly important to recognise this today when capitalism's ideological offensive has made it virtually obligatory to decry class categories as somehow old-fashioned, deserving of being dismissed in favour supposedly more relevant, certainly in-fashion, categories of 'race', 'gender', 'caste', 'ethnicity' etc. At best, class is just another category jostling with these for attention. Class is even reduced in laundry-list fashion to 'classism' alongside racism and sexism, as if it were the result of discriminatory practices directed against a particular section of people. All struggles are or may be on par, but 'identity politics', not class struggle, is the thing for our times, to be practised and to be theorised. Such is the power of this ideological offensive that even among Marxists there are not a few who, wanting to stage a respectable and streamlined reappearance in the field of intellectual debate and practical politics, are only too willing to jettison 'class' and 'class struggle' as dangerous and disposable 'Stalinist' theoretical baggage from the past. Enough for them if it is conceded that class is one identity among many, class struggle is one site among many, and its goal of social transformation is one of many such goals. Class and class struggle are relegated to the status of simply one factor among many, leading to a kind of causal pluralism characteristic of much 'post-modernist' social theory in which everything causes everything and nothing is accorded special explanatory and therefore also political importance – a situation of 'indeterminate multiplicity' of thought and action whose conservative, even reactionary implications are only too obvious. Even otherwise, it needs to be noted, the system has an important vested interest in distorting the categories whereby we think and act. It surely helps to replace 'class' with 'identity' and 'class struggle' with 'identity politics.' The new categories rule out any radical questioning of the system and are eminently adaptable to the requirements of liberal or conservative politics. The new categories, however, have not prevented the ruling classes from a ruthless pursuit of their interests, wreaking what a scholar, Lembcke, has described as 'political-economic devastation seldom seen in history'. At the end of it all, it is turning out to be class struggle for the rich, identity politics for the poor.

XIV

A central question for any strategy of socialist transformation is the question of agency, the social forces that will carry out this transformation. Classical Marxist view of struggle for socialism as class struggle, properly interpreted, carries within it the basic elements of the answer to this question.

It was characteristic of Marxism that even as it established the necessity and possibility of socialism in the material objective conditions first created for it by capitalism, it also looked for the social forces in society that can provide the decisive thrust to the struggle for the new historic form to be achieved. Marx, on the basis of his analysis of capitalism in Western Europe, located this social force, the revolutionary subject or agency, above all in the proletariat of what were in his time the most advanced capitalist countries. Not because any class teleology or metaphysics was involved or, in Marx's words, because 'socialists considered the proletarians as *gods*'. But for the simple reason that as a class of the worst victims of capitalism which 'cannot free itself without abolishing the conditions of its own life', the proletariat was seen to have a most direct objective interest in transition to socialism, and because it was thought natural and easy for it to 'win the theoretical awareness of its loss', that is, acquire the revolutionary consciousness necessary for carrying out this transition. The growing numerical strength of the proletariat as well as its structural location in capitalism, at the very heart of production, was seen to give it a certain strategic social power and capacity for collective action to be an agent of revolutionary transformation. While Marx never denied the role of other social forces in the revolutionary process, indeed sought them as allies of the proletariat, it was the proletariat, the objective situation reinforcing its self-awareness as the prime victim of capitalism and its sense of collective power, which was to be *the* strategic actor in the socialist revolution, 'the grave diggers' of capitalism as Marx called them.

The early struggles of the proletariat and its later role in the October Revolution under Bolshevik leadership and in the post-first world war revolutionary upheaval in Europe vindicated Marx's hopes for the proletariat. But on the whole and in a long-term perspective the European proletariat has not lived up to his expectations. In retrospect Marx can be said to have overestimated the revolutionary potential of the European proletariat, just as he certainly underestimated developmental potential of capitalism and its resilience (via the 'welfare state', etc.) in meeting the challenge of socialism. The western proletariat soon ceased to be the worst victim of capitalist exploitation and failing to 'win the theoretical awareness of its loss' succumbed to bourgeois ideology. 'Economism' turned out to be far more natural and easy in the movement and the expanded role of bourgeois ideology took care of the rest. The proletariat simply could not become, as Marx had hoped, 'a class-for-itself', the revolutionary proletariat. The formation of revolutionary class consciousness indeed turned out to be a far more complex and difficult affair than Marx had visualised. As Ralph Miliband has written: 'Marx and later Marxists [were] far too optimistic in relying on the class location of wage-earners to produce a 'class consciousness' that would obliterate all divisions among them. This quite clearly greatly underestimated the strength of these divisions; and it also failed to take account of what might be called an epistemic dimension, meaning that it is a great deal easier to attribute social ills to Jews, black people, immigrants, other ethnic or religious groups than to a social system and to the men who run it and who are of the same nationality, ethnicity, or religion. To acquire *this* class consciousness requires a mental leap which many people in the working class (and beyond) have performed, but which many other people, subject to intense obfuscation, have not... Class location produces a consciousness which is much more complex and wayward than Marxism assumed; for it leads to reactionary positions as well as progressive ones...'

We have already noticed these and other important causes, objective as well as subjective in nature, behind the proletariat failing socialism in the advanced capitalist countries of the world, so far. It is important to recognise however that these causes are all essentially contingent or conjunctural, a product of the past development of capitalism and the proletariat in the west, which may not always be at work in future. Therefore, it can be legitimately suggested that the problematic of this failure lies not in Marx being wrong but in posing anew the question of this proletariat rediscovering its historically assigned revolutionary role.

The critics, however, have been rather sceptical, denying not only such a possibility but even the existence of classes with antagonistic interests, as Marx saw them, in modern capitalist society. Its past failures apart, they point to the current lack of unity and independence of the working class, a class in which the industrial proletariat has a much diminished presence, which is deeply segmented and differentiated within, fragmented nationally and divided internationally by capitalism through use of racism, sexism, national-chauvinism and such other factors, and marginalised by the cut back of its organisational and legal powers. All this together with 'the changing colours of the cultures' of workers under bourgeois ideological domination, make the working class an altogether unreliable agents of any radical or revolutionary change. Many critics even on the left – Marcuse is a prime example – have argued that the new kind of culture spawned by 'welfare' or 'consumer' capitalism has cast an irrevocable spell on the 'masses', particularly the working class, which has left it bereft of the revolutionary potential it once had. C. Wright Mills, in his time had urged the left to abandon the 'labor metaphysic', and he was certainly not alone in thinking that the working class was no longer available as an oppositional force. Marcuse himself now sought it in students and intellectuals. It is pointed out that the working class is now a declining social force and that other forms of social identity are acquiring a greater salience than those based on class. Even as the growing importance of the 'new middle class' is emphasised, it is regularly suggested that social classes in the old nineteenth-century sense no longer exist as such, especially in the new multinational division of labour, or in the newly automated and cybernetic industries of our post-modern times. Classes and class antagonisms in Marxian sense, critics say, are now things of the past and obituaries abound in sociological literature about the 'death' of class in modern capitalist society. Instead of recognising that what we have here is a rather difficult and complicated problem which can and needs to be resolved and overcome, even well-meaning critics have dismissed Marx's entire perspective as 'wholly misconceived', and writing it off as a revolutionary force said their 'farewell to the working class'.

Critics' views do have a certain validity at the level of detail and it is of course wrong to assign any messianic role to the working class. But their argument as a whole is a mistaken assessment of the situation, mistaken not only about the disappearance of class and class antagonisms in Marxian sense in modern capitalist society but also in writing off the revolutionary potential of the working class, where critics are really a case of replacing one metaphysical imputation (working class in *itself* a saviour of humanity) with its opposite (working class entirely incapable of shaping its own destiny).

I don't think I need to argue anew about the existence of classes and class antagonisms in today's capitalist societies. As visualised in classical Marxist theory, capitalism continues to generate wealth and poverty at two ends of society, polarising it and producing antagonism within, in the advanced capitalist economies as much as in the less advanced ones. This polarisation is today everywhere marked by a sharp increase of inequality and rising levels of absolute poverty in society. Marxist analysis of the tendency for capital to intensify the rates of exploitation under competitive pressures is being borne out, most visibly in the advanced capitalist economies, by the dismantling of the 'welfare state' and the declining share of income accruing to labour as against capital, with labour increasingly transformed into temporary labour, burdened with the increasing costs of social reproduction, increasing costs of health care, loss of pension, etc. Unemployment has became chronic and as wealth is accumulated in the hands of a few at the top, tens of millions of unemployed below, capital's reserve army of labour, are living out their wretched existence on the dole. About the situation in the capitalist societies of the third world, the less said the better.

Classes and class antagonisms remain what they have always been – permanent and dominant realities in modern capitalist societies. What however needs to be particularly noticed in the immediate context is that dynamics of capitalist exploitation, its accumulative logic, along with polarisation also necessarily unleashes a process of proletarianisation in society that confronts capital with its opposite, the wage-dependent proletariat or working class. More than one scholar has pointed out the tendency in recent years for capitalist development to extend wage labour relations in society – salaried professionals, incorporation of woman, expropriation of farmers, expansion of services sector, etc. – with low-paid wage workers increasingly dominating the labour force; three quarters of the new jobs in the capitalist world are of a temporary, low paid, low skill service variety.

It is an unwarranted limitation of the meaning of 'working class' to confine it only to workers in the industrial or manufacturing sector, to factory, manual or blue-collar workers, or to impoverished workers as is done sometimes. The crucial factor is not working in a factory, or working with your hands, or just being poor. All these things can change with fluctuating supply and demand and changing technology and politics. This is indeed how working class has been changing, especially over the past half-century or so, to become the more inclusive social category it is today. The crucial reality is the need to sell your labour to capital in order to live. The decline of employment in the traditional basic industries – steel, coal, autos, etc. – does not mean the end of the working class in a country where the overwhelming majority of the people still live by selling their labour power. Strictly speaking the industrial proletariat is a class fraction. The working class includes all wage earners who live by selling their labour and who do not exercise control over production. Thus it includes the vast majority of the population of advanced capitalist countries, including many who do not recognise themselves as belonging to the working class, or hesitate or refuse to do so, until they are laid off or fired, or 'deskilled', 'outsourced', or 'downsized' – with scholars left fascinated by 'how many of these crushing words are quite new'.

It is true that this more inclusive, 'recomposed' or 'reconstituted' working class is made up of diverse elements; it is much divided and fragmented, with mass entry or re-entry of women into the labour force and changing patterns of migrations, along with the usual divisions and those specific to different countries. But this is nothing new. Division and differences of one kind or another (for example, along skill, sector and gender lines) have always been there in the working class. Marx himself had noted that: 'The division of labour implies from the outset the division of the conditions of labour, of tools and materials, and thus the fragmentation of accumulated capital among different owners, and thus, also, the fragmentation between capital and labour, and the different forms of property itself. The more the division of labour develops and accumulation grows, the further fragmentation develops. Labour itself can only exist on the premise of this fragmentation.' Marx had postulated that the working class had the potentiality to overcome its fragmentation; though, it must be added, he underestimated the practical constraints. The actualisation of the potentiality involved important issues of revolutionary politics – political organisation and socialist consciousness, to mention two of the most important – which remained inadequately addressed by him. These were later more adequately addressed by his followers, noticeably by Lenin and Gramsci, by the former with spectacular success in the Tsarist Russia.

The potentiality postulated by Marx is not to be discounted. The notion of 'working class' still has the 'heuristic' value it had in the past in bringing disparate groups together. Capitalism in its constant recomposition of the working class has regularly divided and redivided that class in various ways. It has always been the task of revolutionary class politics to create unity out of these divisions and differences in the working class. This remains its task today, which has now also to take care of problems posed by 'new social movements' and 'politics of identity'. Arguing that 'if the processes of class fragmentation have today been intensified and expanded, then the effort to create unity out of differences has to be intensified and expanded too', Ellen Neiksins Wood has written: 'This means, among other things, that class organisations have to be more attuned than ever before to "special oppressions" – especially racial and sexual oppressions – and more involved in the struggles against them, both because these struggles are important in themselves and because they are necessary to the construction of class solidarity. So to me the current fragmentation of the working class doesn't mean that we live in an entirely new era in which the "politics of identity" has to replace the politics of class. On the contrary, it means that, in the face of a "totalising" capitalist system, the main organizational energies of the left must now more than ever be devoted to constructing a unified class politics on the local and national level.'

Again, it is true that most of this working class never has been revolutionary in Marx's sense. But sections of it have taken part in revolutionary struggles and even made revolutions, and its divisions have not prevented a large part of it from quite frequently supporting radical programmes of social renewal. That these programmes have not been carried out cannot be attributed to the failings of the working class itself. No doubt there is a profound gap today between 'class-in-itself' and 'class-for-itself', between the objective expansion of the working class and the development of forms of organisation and consciousness capable of effectively articulating and defending its interests and playing the role Marx saw for it in the social transformation of society. But vital working class movements have come up in different countries in recent years. Europe itself – in France, Italy, Germany and elsewhere – has witnessed mass strikes and militant class actions indicative of the revolutionary potential of the working class. This is how an observer, Raghu Krishnan, reported on the great strike movement against the Juppe government in France in 1995:

> Participants in December's strikes and protests in France sent an important message to the world: yes, the working class does in fact exist. From the 1980s onwards, we have been treated to all sorts of ideological nonsense about how the working class in the industrialized countries was no more. We were headed into a 'new age' where work would be done by computers and everyone else would simply have to figure out what to do with their 'leisure time' 'Surfing' the Internet? 'Eco-tourism' in Brazil? 'Virtual reality' video games and sex? 'Cyber-shopping' from home? The choices would be endless and available to all in the 'new age of prosperity.' However, it turns out that ordinary people continue to do the work, and that those with excess 'leisure time' are usually the millions who have been unceremoniously kicked out of the labour force, who have never even been in it, or who have low-wage, part-time, unstable jobs.
>
> Politics and culture in this luckless era of ours have effectively 'forgotten' that the majority of people's adult lives are spent at work – or in search of it, as the case may be. In addition to being stuck doing boring, tiring, and repetitive tasks, working people must also put up with an insufferably authoritarian climate of fear and suspicion on the job – made all the worse by the constant threat of unemployment.
>
> One observer noted that the December events in France signalled not only the existence of a classical working class – defined as those who must sell their labour power to survive – but also that this working class occupies a clear majority position within French society. The protest movement underlined the basic unity and mass character of labour in the country. Out of the movement emerged a working-class identity and a sense that workers in France are at a crossroads, as were U.S. workers at the time of the air traffic controllers strike under Ronald Reagan and British workers at the time of the miners strike under Margaret Thatcher.
>
> One thing is certain. The events in France show that a movement based on the workplace and its relation in society will be a key component of any democratic regeneration and any re-emergence of passion and creativity in our societies.

All this is only to suggest that not only is working class very much there, it remains a victim of capitalist exploitation and retains its radical potentialities. It is necessary to take a critical but balanced view of its situation in the current phase of development of capitalism. The need is not to dismiss but reclaim the changed and changing working class for the socialist project in the light of present reality, taking into account the new structure of the working class (with its many women and immigrants), the growing number of white collar workers, the international recomposition of the industrial working class, the new role played by science in production, etc., and above all the structural tendencies towards unification of the working class for all the factors that fragment, divide or disperse it. Quiescence of the working class is not an innate characteristic as is not revolutionary impulses. The possibility of renewal of working class radicalism and the formation around it of a bloc capable of long-term dynamic action is always there. The task is to mount an ideological and organisational political effort to realise this possibility.

Understood as a part of his overall view of the struggle for socialism, Marx's perspective on the role of working class in this struggle, far from being 'misconceived' or 'exhausted' as the critics have contended, still holds. When Marx wrote of the proletariat in the *Communist Manifesto* (1848), it was still only a minority in most European societies, not to mention the rest of the world. Today, the mass of wage-workers exploited by capital – industrial workers, white-collar workers, service workers, day labourers, farmhands – comprises the majority of the world's population. While specificities of the class situation in each country has always to be taken into account, it is today potentially the most important force in the struggle against the global capitalist system, the axis around which other social struggles can and must orient themselves.

These considerations are broadly relevant to the working class in every country where it has a significant presence, whatever be the specificities of its historical development and the present situation. As victims of capitalism, local or globalised, as regards their 'necessarily subordinate location in the command structure of capital', there is essentially no difference between the workers of the 'underdeveloped' countries and their counterparts in the most privileged capitalist countries. To this one may add that post-decolonisation, the industrialisation of significant parts of the third world, notably in East and South Asia, and in Latin-America, has substantially increased the number of wage-labourers, and even otherwise the process of proletarianisation in the third-world continues. Globalisation as a project which Marx once described as 'the entanglement of all peoples in the net of the world market', also aims at delivering an exploited global proletariat into the hands of capitalism – 'drawing the poorest of the world's population into the work force to create a reserve army of labour that will enforce the disciplines of capitalist labour-markets across the greater part of humanity', as Paul Cammack has described it. This will only add to Frantz Fanon's 'wretched of the earth', already a majority of the third world population, who are the real successors of the proletariat of Marx's time and whose interests are quintessentially the same as those of the proletariat everywhere. The question of ripeness of conditions for it notwithstanding, history of our times has put socialism on the agenda of future progress everywhere. The third world working class and its allies, especially the poor peasantry and the landless, whose revolutionary potential is not to be underestimated, are the key social forces today for a socialism-oriented transformation of their societies. The task for socialists, here as elsewhere is to undertake a careful class analysis of their society, locate the prime victims of its class exploitation as the basic revolutionary social forces, help them 'win the theoretical awareness of (their) loss', that is acquire revolutionary consciousness, provide them with appropriate programmes and organisation and structure around the basic forces a bloc of other strata and movements committed to radical change in society. Most important is the practice of independent class politics. Independence here alone ensures that alliances, even compromises, with other classes or strata which pursuit of independent class politics never excludes, advance the revolutionary cause and not end up as tailist exercises.

It is to be noted that even as he focused on the working class as the core constituency of socialism, Marx recognised the important role of other strata or classes, especially the intellectuals and peasants, in the revolutionary process. He wrote of sections of old society especially intellectuals 'who have raised themselves to the level of comprehending theoretically the historical movement as a whole', 'going over to the proletariat', and of 'the country people who want to overthrow the old order by their own energies, in alliance with the towns'. Writing of 'class struggles in France', he had said: 'The French workers could not take a step forward, could not touch a hair of the bourgeois order, until the course of the revolution had aroused the mass of the nation, the peasants and petty bourgeois standing between the proletariat and the bourgeoisie, against this order, against the rule of capital, and had forced them to attach themselves to the proletarians as their protagonists.' Marx recognised not only 'the (conservative) peasant who wants to consolidate the condition of his social existence, the small holding', but also 'the revolutionary peasant... who strikes out beyond it' for a different, better future. (The peasant, Bolshevik Kalinin was to say later, possesses 'two souls': one of a proprietor, and the other of a worker.) While 'the bigger peasants belong to the bourgeoisie', Engels considered 'the small peasant who does his own work as virtually belonging to us'. Marx's focus on proletariat was never exclusionary. He envisaged and sought allies for the working class, especially in the peasantry. Marx noticed how 'Paris' was regularly defeated by 'France' and stressed the need for the proletariat to have the peasantry on its side instead of its being, passively or otherwise, on the side of the bourgeoisie. He had insisted that something akin to 'Peasant War in Germany' was a precondition for the success of any 'proletarian revolution' in France. And not only in France. In 1956, he wrote to Engels: 'The whole thing in Germany will depend on the possibility of backing the proletarian revolution by some second edition of the Peasant War.' I have touched on this issue earlier. I will only again add that Marx visualised 'the proletarian movement' as the 'movement of the immense majority, in the interest of the immense majority'.

Abstracted from its specific context, the argument underlying Marx's perspective is in fact suggestive of a wider constituency for socialism, much wider today than ever before. 'Privileging' is a word commonly used to describe Marx's focus on the role of the working class in the struggle against capitalism. This is a rather loaded term, one easily amenable to a reductionist interpretation. Marxism certainly rejects the post-modernist notions of 'the discursive formation of identity' or 'causal indeterminacy'. But no reductionist or determinist original sin is involved in its assessment of the role of the working class. It is not an arbitrary assessment and it does not mean 'privileging' one set of actors over others, or seeing the working class as the *only agent*, and its class struggle *the only site* of struggle against capitalism. For Marx there is no 'chosen class' any more than there can be a 'chosen people' in history. Marx assigned the role he did to the working class not because he considered the proletarians as *gods*' or because 'gods have said so', as he himself categorically stated, but for good 'earthly' reasons. What is essentially involved in Marx' perspective is the elementary sociological notion of identities, interests and possibilities of action being grounded in structural social position. Surely it is legitimate to argue that the victims of oppressive social relations have a credible interest in changing them and are more likely to organise and act in order to change them. Marx himself saw the working class of his time as the worst victim of capitalism – which indeed it was – and focussed on its objective interest in changing this system – which it indeed had. But this has no implications of such interest being necessarily or exclusively confined to the working class. Other classes, strata or individuals may, or may come to, share in this interest. Even if not its worst victims they may yet find capitalism an objectionable system, one needing to be replaced by a better social order --- and thus become a real or potential constituency for socialism.

Marx wrote not only of capitalism's 'naked, shameless, direct, brutal exploitation' of workers, 'the direct producers of surplus value', but also of how capitalism ravages everything human or natural that comes under its sway. His ethical-aesthetic critique of capitalism pointed out how logic of 'the market' distorts and diminishes human beings in capitalist society. Who can deny the truth, then or now, of the passage in *Communist Manifesto* where Marx describes what bourgeois society forces people to be, that is, become brutal in order to survive in the cold-blooded world of capitalism: In the course of 'pitilessly tearing asunder the motley feudal ties', bourgeois society, 'has left remaining no other nexus between man and man than naked self-interest, than callous "cash payment"'. It has 'drowned' every form of sentimental value 'in the icy water of egotistical calculation'. It has 'resolved personal worth into exchange-value'. It has collapsed every historical tradition and norm of freedom 'into that single, unconscionable freedom – free trade', and so on. Obviously, given the material and moral devastation wrought by capitalism, people other than workers can and do have interest in changing the capitalist social order. The constituency for socialism is not necessarily confined to only the working class.

We continue to live under capitalism, which is as exploitative as ever and even more destructive of our social, physical and psychological space. Become truly global, it has drawn the whole world into the orbit of its systemic contradictions, reproducing on a global scale its original logic of dispossession and polarisation. A very wide range of oppressions apart from class exploitation – racial, gender, national or ethnic and many more – which intersect with and are reinforced by capitalist exploitation are surfacing as never before. The power of capital has come to be exercised, openly or in diffused fashion, in all areas of life and its material and moral-cultural depredations are becoming daily more visible everywhere. The constituency for socialism is, therefore, today much wider than it has been for a long time. Indeed it is not only strictly proletarian interests that are at stake today, it is all oppressed social categories and groups – women, tribals, dalits, nations and ethnic groups under alien domination, the unemployed and marginalised (the 'proletariat') – of all countries, and all those wanting a life worthy of human beings on this earth who now have a stake in socialist transformation of society. And this without raising the question of the environment which concerns the human species as a whole and where the future of earth itself is at stake. In the face of the ecological destruction inevitably caused by the accumulation-driven system that is capitalism, socialism is no longer (if it ever was) a mere utopian dream – it is today a necessary defence of humanity and the earth.

Capitalism, though globally dominant, is today a crisis-ridden, materially, morally and culturally sick social order, finding its victims in all sections of society, oppressing people in a hundred different ways. Everywhere there is deep discontent with the way the things are, a search for a different, better way of life. All kinds of big or small protests and initiatives are emerging, questioning different aspects of the prevalent social order. The hitherto repressed 'underground tendencies' as Lukacs called them, are wanting to be liberated and people are beginning to move into action in defence of their interests. If the individuals, groups, strata and classes could be persuaded to see the linkages or interconnections of their concerns with the predatory logic of capitalism, the possibility is very much there for a coalition of social forces around the basic classes upon which struggle for socialism can be based.

In considering the human resources available for the resumed struggle for socialism, we must not underestimate socialism's natural constituency as a moral ideal. Throughout history people have been moved by moral considerations to oppose oppression and fight for a better life for all. So it has been in the struggle for socialism. Men and women with democratic and humanist sensibilities have in the past rejected capitalism as an unjust and immoral social order and stood by those fighting for socialism. They can do so in the present and the future. In fact socialism itself has always had an ethical concern underlying it. Motivation flowing from 'objective material interests' has of course been important but the socialist demand for a revolutionary transformation of society was always essentially motivated by ethical considerations. A commitment in behalf of humanity has always been the driving force behind the socialist project.

This commitment is clearly expressed in Marx when early in his life he put 'working for humanity' at the centre of his values for life and endorsed 'the categorical imperative to overthrow all conditions in which man is a humiliated, enslaved, despised and rejected being'. This remained the motivating commitment in the revolutionary socialist movement throughout, finding equally eloquent expression in Lenin and Mao, in Che Guevara, and of course Rosa Luxemburg for whom 'all conditions based on social inequality are fundamentally abnormal', who wrote of bourgeois society that 'its innermost law of life is the profoundist of immoralities, namely, te exploiation of man by man', and wo saw 'the proletariat' as 'qualified to uproot thousand-year-old oaks of social injustice'. It may be added that the alternative socialism seeks is not a class alternative, but an alternative for all humanity. Even though the struggle for them is saturated with class, the ends socialists seek are tangentially universal: the freedom of each and the freedom of all. As Marx and Engels put it in the *Communist Manifesto:* 'In place of the old bourgeois society, with its classes and class antagonisms, we shall have an association in which free development of each is the condition for the free development of al.'

The thical basis and ends of socialism link the struggle for socialism, its exceptional historically-given specificity notwithstanding, to humankind's persistent struggle against oppression and exploitation and for a more humane social order. Victor G. Kiernan has written: 'Every social struggle or movement has also been a moral issue over which individuals took risks for the sake of their fellows. Resistance to oppression has not only speeded up technical progress, but has builtmankind's moral reserves, its accumulation of moral capital'. In our time, socialists, especially as communists, have contributed immensely to the building of this 'moral capital' of humankind. They can surely bank on it and legitimately hope that socialism will continue to win adherents as a moral ideal.

XV

An important problem confronting the struggle for socialism today is that posed by 'new social movements', and associated phenomena springing from 'civil society' as it is called, which are among the more significant developments of recent decades and are often viewed as the prime agents of social transformation in our times. Described variously these are: the feminist, ecological, civil rights, peace and anti-nuclear movements; movements based on identities other than class and against oppressions having to do with age, race, gender and sexuality, ethnicity, nationality or religion, or a combination of these; struggles of the long oppressed and more disadvantaged sections like women, dalits and tribals, minor nationalities or ethnic groups, racial and religions minorities; communitarian movements (with their yearning for 'community', 'family values' and 'spiritual civilisation'); a wide variety of voluntary activism and non-governmental organisations (NGOs); all kinds of 'grass-roots' movements, libertarian leftism and political activism including 'politics of the street' which has seen the emergence of numerous marginal groups preaching self-management, local control, politics of personal transformation and decentralisation, and so on. Of these, 'new social movements' are of course the most important, with the issues raised by the associated concept of 'civil society' and such other significant phenomena as 'NGOs' and 'identity politics' very much a part of the argument over the social movements.

The 'new social movements' have a long history; some, including the feminist and peace movements, have roots going back at least to the early decades of the twentieth century. (Becoming prominent, or re-emerging, in renewed and more militant form in the 1970s and 1980s in the pan-European part of global capitalist system, they are now a worldwide development.) They are 'new' in the sense that they are seen to typify the 'political' in 'post-modern' or 'post-organised' capitalist societies. The theorising over them has a distinct 'post-Marxist' or 'post-modern', that is essentially anti-Left, flavour about it, including a tendency to deny the importance of general theorising. These movements are claimed to have displaced the Marxist-led class movement or struggle from its central strategic role in opposing the present-day social order so much so that an Aranson has even proclaimed: 'Feminism killed Marxism'. Sociologist Alain Touraine has argued that the new social movements are the harbingers of new forms of protest appropriate to a post-industrial society in which new middle strata have replaced workers as the location of progressive action. Even when some fragments of these movements have claimed to be anti-capitalist, in most cases they have seen their struggles as transcending 'older' debates about capitalism altogether. Habermasian analyses, as a critic has pointed out, have made new social movements out to be 'the vanguard of struggle to sustain the "life world" against colonization by "the system", while classifying workers' organizations as part of the latter'. Post-modernists, denouncing socialism as a 'meta-narrative' that is inevitably totalitarian, have hailed them as evidence of what alone is permissible or possible today – their preferred politics of 'diversity', 'difference' and 'identity', – and provided them with the requisite theoretical support.

Though challenging the existing order of things and as a whole potentially anti-capitalist, these social movements themselves have shown a marked antipathy to the Left. Partly because the working classes' lack of credibility as general emancipators in our time has often led them to define themselves in opposition to the working class and partly also because of Left's 'big brotherly' attitude, its misconceived propensity to translate the concerns of others into its own terms and the indifferent or hostile manner in which some lefts have tended to treat them. The crisis on the Left which followed the collapse in the Soviet Union has only strengthened their conviction of the irrelevance of the Left, of its politics based on class.

Abandoning the concept of class and class politics, now held to be theoretically and practically overburdened, if not altogether mistaken, new social movements have opted for an alternative politics whose terrain is 'civil society', constituted by all sorts of 'diversity' and 'difference' or 'identities', where 'pluralism' as it is called, is asking for recognition and acceptance in theory and practice of any kind of radicalism, and where class is, at best, only one among the many identities, with no structural or any other privileges. Marxism is jettisoned for a systems analysis of state and civil society abstracted from the economic context, and only 'new social movements', including struggles of 'identities', are expected to provide an effective challenge to the status quo, which the traditional labour and socialist movement, too steeped in ancient (and obsolete) modes of thought and action can never do. The primacy of class politics is rejected in favour of 'democratic struggles', especially as they are conducted by the 'new social movements' and by an ideology autonomous of any class determination or affiliation. Socialist concepts of 'classes' and 'masses' 'deconstructed' and jettisoned, the vocabulary of politics today is flush with terms like 'collective identity', 'identity groups', 'identity politics' or, for that matter, 'ethnicity' and 'oppressed categories', with cultural factors given the place of honour. In the 'post-socialist' conflicts of our time, group identity supplants class interest as the chief medium of political mobilisation. Cultural domination supplants exploitation as the fundamental injustice. And cultural recognition displaces socio-economic redistribution as the remedy for injustice and the goal of struggle. The 'struggle for recognition' has indeed become the paradigmatic form of political conflict today. It is the demand for 'recognition of difference' that fuels struggles of groups mobilised under the banners of nationality, ethnicity, race, gender, and sexuality. Even a 'Do-it-Yourself (DIY) politics has arrived in preference to class and mass politics of yester years.

Even on the Left, there are not a few who, in their present state of loss of confidence in the traditional socialist ideas and agencies of change, and swinging away from the old economistic practices, are succumbing to the class-free politics of 'civil society', not realising that in failing to recognise the overarching totality of capitalism as a system that shapes all politics in society, sets the range of its possibilities and outcomes, this politics begs the entire question of capitalism, and that opting for this politics ultimately amounts to a retreat from the search and the striving for a socialist alternative to capitalism. Some are even urging upon us the need today to think and act as a 'global civil society', little realising that this is simply being the dialectical twins of those who preach that globalisation has ended all alternatives to capitalism.

The 'new social movements' have sprung from real sources within capitalist society, reflecting its major concerns like ecology or feminism, its continuing problems of poverty, inequality and social injustice or plain anguish of large sections of people victimised by the dynamics of late capitalism worldwide, at the centre and in the peripheries. Influenced by the failure both of social democracy and Soviet communism, they also reflect a growing lack of faith in the state as the agent of social improvement, accompanied by deep frustration with the existing parties and political system, its so-called power of vote and democratic procedures. 'Ethnicity' or 'identity' has been with us for quite sometime now as a consequence of the upheavals and transformations of society, the dissolution of traditional social norms, textures and values that have accompanied the development of capitalism at home and abroad. The weakening of the state and the old class-based political parties and movements together with the massive dislocation of people set in motion by capitalist restructuring of recent years has only intensified people's need and search for 'identity'. As Hobsbawm has put it: 'Men and women look for groups to which they can belong, certainly and forever, in a world in which all else is moving and shifting, in which nothing else is certain. And they find it in an identity group.' Given the all too obvious failures and frustrations of contemporary 'mainstream' politics, it is but one small step from this to the 'politics of identity'.

Socialists however need to acknowledge that 'new social movements', the way they have emerged, are not only direct or indirect products of the economy and politics of the capitalist social order but are also born of dissatisfaction with the limitations of traditional communist or socialist movements and parties, drawing attention to various important issues inadequately addressed by them. There is no denying that these movements and parties, including those claiming to be guided by Marxism, have long suffered from 'economism' for which the only source of real discontent is economic exploitation, here alone real dissent and challenge to the system can arise, and socialism is more than anything else about economics and economic welfare. Issues like feminism and ecology have always had trouble finding a really significant place in Marxist political discourse or party programmes, and the organised movement has generally been averse to accepting that it can learn anything important from contemporary social movements. It is not that issues of concern to these movements have been entirely missing. But even when taken seriously, the tendency has been to translate them into party's own terms, to redefine them for incorporation into its own socialist discourse. 'More often than not', George Ross has written, 'the result was that these issues were subordinated by the Left to "more important" matters of class and class conflict. Women's issues were a case in point. Whatever the initial form of their expression, the Left had usually translated them into the concerns of women *workers*. Similarly, environmental matters were often subordinated to the Left's productivism. Issues involving the so-called private sphere were either collectivized or dismissed as petit bourgeois individualism. Peace issues were often subordinated to Cold War mapping of international class struggle.' The issues thus remained essentially unaddressed. It is disenchantment with such conventional 'class politics' which explains the attraction of 'new politics' of the social movements even for certain sections of the Left. It is not enough to point to Marx's criticism of environmental destruction, or the pioneering feminism of Engels, or Marxist participation over the years in ecological and feminist struggles. The fact remains that the organised socialist or communist movements, as they have existed in reality, have been mostly indifferent, if not unsympathetic to ecology, feminism, and similar other less-exclusively class-functional concerns, and are the poorer for that. Whatever their own limitations in keeping away from the insights of Marxism, the new social movements have drawn attention to an important limitation of the organised Marxist movements which needs to be frankly acknowledged and overcome. Socialists have to have a deep-seated commitment to all forms of human emancipation, and this commitment has to be not formally but genuinely and creatively built into their theory and political programmes.

It is fashionable these days to trace the limitations of the

Marxist-led movements to Marx himself, to his mistaken theories. So it is now with the above-mentioned limitation. It is traced to Marx's theory of class and class struggle. Marx is charged with 'reductionism', which ignores the complexity of social life and reduces all struggles to that of class. The theory is also seen as the source of Marxists' propensity to establish an indefensible hegemony over the definition of radicalism or progressive politics which brings them inevitably into conflict with new social movements. Such charges however are nothing more than 'straw-Marxist' arguments. Marx was a historical materialist and his theory of class and class struggle involves no reductionism. To accept Marx is not to deny or diminish the importance of environmentalism, feminism, or anti-racism (or of anti-dalitism in India). Rather, it is to place the corresponding negative or oppressive behaviours in their larger social and historical context and to see how these have now become bound up – in whatever complex ways – not only with each other but also, more fundamentally, with the priorities of capitalism. The awareness of class, with Marx, offers a scaffolding for common struggles against the multiple oppressions of the capitalist social order. Ironically, it is those who berate Marxist 'reductionism' who end up confining people to categories they cannot transcend.

Marx's theory, of course, has its limitations or gaps, 'silences' and 'empty spaces', as it pertains to non-class identities and concerns. Critics, inclined to be generous, have often traced them to his location in the nineteenth century which made him share many of the now-outdated ideas and assumptions of the time in which he lived. Such criticism ignores the fact that the consciousness of capitalism's enormities could not possibly emerge in every dimension at once, even in the mind of system's most prescient critic. That consciousness depended on specific historical processes which came to fruition at different times – in most cases they did so much after Marx. Still more relevant here is another consideration. Implicit in Marx's theory is the view that this only reflects the complexity of capitalism as a system which touches every aspect of human existence. And it was the signal contribution of Marx to lay bare the integrative core of this system, the class exploitation constituting it, which is, however conditionally, determinative of different aspects of the capitalist social order and its other enormities as well. Class as the more basic principle of their organisation, determines and better explains the development and reproduction of contemporary capitalist societies and this includes the emergence of concerns that new social movements have justifiably made their own. What is at issue therefore is *not* whether or not ecological degradation or war, sexism or racism, or diverse identity-based oppressions deserve immediate and focussed attention and action, but rather whether or not they can be effectively dealt with independently of their links to capitalism or its abolition. Socialism would of course not solve all the predicaments of the human race; there are sufferings and oppressions beyond class, many of which may have an earlier origin and greater tenacity than class oppression and domination. A transition from capitalism to socialism would not automatically eliminate them. But it remains a necessary condition for their elimination. Marxism with its focus on class and class exploitation seeks to tackle these and other problems confronting society from the right end. And no better guide is available.

There is no denying the importance of the new social movements motivated by other than class interests and struggles based on identities other than class, and their significant achievements in behalf of the people. They have drawn our attention to grave problems like ecological degradation and, as against the conventional focus on economic oppression, identified and challenged other long obscured or neglected oppressions – oppressions 'hidden from history' in Sheila Rowbotham's words. The groups or identities concerned have been victims of double oppression – the class oppression which affects the exploited everywhere and the oppressions specific to each group or identity. It has been still worse in case of women who, subject to the most ancient of oppressions, have been most vulnerable to exploitation, exclusion, deprivation and violence of the worst kind, and are today a vast oppressed and marginalised majority in the world. Of course we must make a distinction between the various social movements on the basis of their aims, methods and ethics, between those which are a creative contribution to radical politics and are to be welcomed – for example, feminist, ecological, peace and solidarity movements – and those which presage a dangerous future and need to be resisted – for example, racist or religious fundamentalist movements. But this does not take away from the positive significance of the new social movements as a whole. They have underlined the plurality of identities in society and the facts that class cannot capture all its grievances and oppressions, that the many contradictions now emerging in it cannot be reduced to class contradictions, nor all struggles reduced to struggle against class exploitation, that new subjects, new needs and new struggles are emerging and their autonomy must be recognised. All this is very justified and necessary too. No socialist can doubt the importance of diversity, or the multiplicity of oppressions that need to be abolished.

The social movements have in their own way challenged the existing social order and have significant achievements to their credit. They have done valuable work checking particular manifestations of the destructive logic of capitalism, rectifying many wrongs, and securing some justice for the victims of its diverse oppressions. They have contributed to the subversion of many 'accepted' political meanings and cultural values and disturbed the mental status quo of the countries in which they have flowered. Their 'identity politics' has, as for example with Blacks in America or dalits in India, significantly undermined the age-old racial or caste discriminations in society. It may be hopefully assumed that they will continue to advance popular causes and have a positive effect on the political culture and agendas of their societies. Identity politics can be a potentially liberating, even equalising development, especially among subordinate groups. Together with it the new social movements have the potential to be a part of the combination of anti-capitalist agencies or social forces that strive for socialism, and whose consolidation is a primary strategic-political task today. But as they exist today, they are not the agents of social transformation they had promised or set out to be. Deliberately partial and self-limiting, the social movements have been able, at best, to mount only partial and limited rebellions, without challenging directly or indirectly the rule of capital. What remains conspicuously absent in all they do is any sense of what a genuinely alternative politics has to be – they have no clear idea of what they are up against and what they want their societies to be. The ideas or concepts underlying them add up to no emancipatory theory and their practice makes for no emancipatory project.

'An emancipatory theory', Ellen Meiksins Wood has pointed out, 'is more than just a statement of general principles and good intentions. It also involves a critical view of the world as it is, a map of the existing terrain which informs our understanding of the obstacles to be overcome, an insight into the conditions of struggle. And an emancipatory theory takes us beyond the limiting and mystifying ideological categories which support existing dominations and oppressions.' The theory which claims to speak for the new social movements – working with the concepts of 'civil society', 'identity', 'pluralism', etc. – simply does not fit the bill. Instead it is essentially anti-emancipatory. Its concern with 'identity' and 'pluralism', reduces the whole system of capitalism to one set of institutions and relations among many other that constitute 'civil society', on a conceptual par with households or voluntary associations. The entire problem of capitalism is conceptualised away by disaggregating society into fragments, with no over-arching power structure, no totalising unity, no systemic coercions – in other words, no capitalist system, with its expansionary drive and its capacity to penetrate every aspect of social life. Such theorising obviously cannot make for any kind of emancipatory practice in contemporary capitalist society. As it is, the new social movements do not reflect, are not intended to create, a new collective identity, a new social agency, motivated by a new anti-capitalist interest which dissolves differences of class interest. They are not constituted on the basis of a recognition of the connections that exist between the capitalist order and its diverse non-class oppressions or, for example, between this order and the current threats to peace or human survival on this earth. Instead, their unity and popular appeal have depended upon abstracting these issues from the prevailing social order and the conflicting social interests that comprise it. The social movements, in short, have no viable framework of reference for understanding the world, no systemic analysis of the structural source of social problems, grievances or oppressions in society. Even if they won sufficient support, what alternative could they offer at the level of regional or national government? Dissatisfied with the present-day social order, what vision of a new society they have which they would develop in its place? They have no answers because they don't pose such questions. They are content to make statements of general principles and good intentions. And in situations of crisis in society, which are becoming all too frequent these days, we have desperate scholars and social activists asking for 'the long-term plan of action of the civil society' – whatever that means. There are even calls for 'the civil society to act *now*, without undue delay'!

The concept of 'civil society' that underlies their theory and practice is really the Achilles' heel of the social movements, responsible for their flawed understanding of capitalism and capitalist society and therefore also for their limitations, and failure so far, as agents of social transformation. A critical look at this concept, therefore, will not be out of place before proceeding with our discussion on social movements and drawing the necessary conclusions from it. (Incidentally, 'civil society' is today the panacea for IMF and the World Bank and, along with 'democracy' it is 'civil society' that American imperialism is busy 'constructing', if necessary with force of arms, in the third world).

'Civil society' is a rather versatile concept with much fuzziness surrounding it. It has a long 'somewhat tortuous history' with important landmarks in the work of Hegel and Marx, and more recently Gramsci (whose argument we have noted earlier). Its principal current usages proceed from the distinction between state and civil society, where the state is at least in principle the site of coercion and civil society is, by definition, the sphere of freedom and voluntary action. The important point for consideration here is the view taken of what constitutes this realm of freedom. The significant anti-thesis underlying the above distinction is state and non-state, rather political and social — and social as 'civil society' includes virtually everything strictly non-state or non-political in society, from family, churches, voluntary associations, social institutions and relations of all sorts to the market, capitalist enterprises, indeed the whole capitalist system. The reduction of capitalist system to one set of institutions and relations among others is in fact the principal distinctive feature of 'civil society' in its current incarnation. Typical of the concept is its positive recognition of 'difference' and 'diversity' of institutions and relations in society, a 'pluralism' which we are invited to appreciate and celebrate. Democracy is tied up with the flourishing of this 'diversity' and 'pluralism', even equated with 'the liberation of civil society'. For the more enthusiastic, human emancipation consists in the autonomy of civil society, its expansion and enrichment, its liberation from the state, and its protection by formal democracy.

The concept of 'civil society' has drawn fresh attention to the need and possibilities of popular participation and intervention in matters of popular concern. It certainly helps towards making us more sensitive to the question of civil liberties, to the need not only of defending them against state oppression but also of strengthening our defence of valuable non-state institutions and relations against the power of the state. Its emphasis on the value of difference and diversity, of pluralism in society, its marking out a terrain of positive social practices, institutions and relations, often neglected by 'old' Marxist left, are both welcome and opportune. Civil society, thus, can indeed be viewed as a space for freedom, that is, for certain forms of freedom and popular action – whose importance is not to be underestimated. But beyond this, 'civil society' is a much-flawed concept. 'Civil society' is not the realm of freedom or democracy its advocates make it out to be. The Taliban, the RSS and the Ku Klux Klan or multinational corporations and Foundations, all such non-state set-ups, are as much part of civil society as small human rights or self-help groups. Civil society is marred by unequal power relations and harsh socio-economic contradictions, by oppressions in the family, in gender relations, in the workplace, by racist, casteist or religious-fundamentalist attitudes and xenophobia. Again, the non-state or private does not necessarily translate as 'free'. The power wielded by capitalist wealth both in the economy and in the political sphere does not exactly make for or add to freedom in society. The process is not 'free' when it is private and is busy 'manufacturing consent' for the powers that be. Indeed one of the principal functions of 'public' coercion by the state is to sustain 'private' power and its coercions in civil society.

As a concept, the most important flaw of 'civil society' lies in its understanding of capitalism and the capitalist social order. It is not only that capitalism is not just another set of relations but a relation of exploitation and domination in civil society and that the coercive functions of the state, rooted in these relations, are in large part occupied with the enforcement of this exploitation and domination in civil society. It is also that these relations of exploitation and domination irreducibly constitute civil society, not as some alien and correctible disorder but as its very essence and that more than a system of exploitation and domination, capitalism is a ruthless totalising process that penetrates into the deepest recesses of public and private life. It subjects all social life to the abstract requirements of the market, commodifies life in all its aspects, determines the allocation of labour and resources, the patterns of production, consumption and disposition of time. This not only makes a mockery of all our aspirations to autonomy and freedom in civil society but also shows up 'pluralism' to be yet another notion of neo-liberal theory that evades, mystifies or conceals the reality of the capitalist social order.

Ellen Meiksins Wood has written:

> The separation of the state and civil society in the West has certainly given rise to new forms of freedom and equality, but it has also created new modes of domination and coercion. One way of characterizing the specificity of 'civil society' as a particular social form unique to the modern world – the particular historical

> conditions which made possible the modern distinction between state and civil society – is to say that it constituted a new form of social power, in which many coercive functions that once belonged to the state were relocated in the 'private' sphere, in private property, class exploitation, and market imperatives. It is, in a sense, this 'privatization' of public power which has created the historically novel realm of 'civil society'. 'Civil society' constitutes not only a wholly new relation between 'public' and 'private' but more precisely a wholly new 'private' realm, with a distinctive 'public' presence and oppressions of its own, a unique structure of power and domination, and a ruthless systemic logic. It represents a particular network of social relations which does not simply stand in opposition to the coercive, 'policing' and 'administrative' functions of the state but represents the *relocation* of these functions, a new division of labour between the 'public' sphere of the state and the 'private' sphere of capitalist property and the imperatives of the market, in which appropriation, exploitation and domination are detached from public authority and social responsibility.
>
> 'Civil society' has given private property and its possessors a command over people and their daily lives, a power accountable to no one, which many an old tyrannical state would have envied. Those activities and experiences which fall outside the immediate command structure of the capitalist enterprise, or outside the political power of capital, are regulated by the dictates of the market, the necessities of competition and profitability. Even when the market is not, as it commonly is in advanced capitalist societies, merely an instrument of power for giant conglomerates and multinational corporations, it is still a coercive force, capable of subjecting all human values, activities and relationships to its imperatives. No ancient despot could have hoped to penetrate the personal lives of his subjects – their choices, preferences, and relationships – in the same comprehensive and minute detail, not only in the workplace but in every corner of their lives. Coercion, in other words, has been not just a *disorder* of 'civil society' but one of its constitutive principles.

'Civil society' is not a realm of freedom, and 'pluralism' is not a true description of how it is in the capitalist social order. Activists of social movements need to recognise the overarching totality of capitalism as a social system, which is constituted by class exploitation, but which shapes *all* 'identities' and social relations in society. Its class relations decisively impact every other aspect of social life and transform and integrate every other oppression into the system as a whole. The effectiveness of social movements, even for their partial or limited purposes, depends on their being part of a larger and wider movement against the system that is capitalism.

This is an argument that can never be overemphasised. As has been pointed out earlier, class relations are not merely a matter of personal identity, or an indicator of inequality, or a principle of stratification, not even a specific system of power relations in society. They are the *constitutive* relations of a distinctive social process, the dynamic of accumulation and self-expression of capital. It is this which gives them the historically determinative force that pluralist identities, institutions or 'spheres' of civil society, even when they are expressive of inequality or domination, do not have. Instead the latter themselves to a most significant degree, come within the determinative force of capitalist class relations, indeed of capitalism as a whole, its system of social property relations, its expansionary imperatives, its drive for accumulation, its commodification of all social life, its creation of the market as a *necessity*, a compulsive mechanism of self sustaining 'growth'. Racial, caste and gender domination, for example, are shaped by the class in which they are embedded more than the forms of class domination are shaped by gender or race or caste. Even sex does not, so to say, speak it own truth, its potentialities or control tracks discoverable by a focus on itself and its discourses, alone. Bodies are not just the property of their occupants, they must also labour and live through exploitation, oppression and alienation. Sex is not just a process in the hands of those who are living or doing it, it is always unfolding itself within a set of determinations, most important of them traceable to the class relations of capitalism today. And love has a parallel history of its own. Class relationships are central to the possibilities of a human condition that reaches beyond many boundaries, those of sexuality among them. That is why attempts at elimination of non-class oppressions must acknowledge the limits and character of change possible within capitalism as a class society.

These oppressions may have equal *moral* claims but class exploitation has a different *historical* status, a more strategic location at the heart of capitalism. Class struggle therefore has a more universal reach, a greater potential for advancing not only class emancipation but other emancipatory struggles too.

The above argument has a corollary which is equally important to be taken note of. It is that class exploitation or class relations are *constitutive* of capitalism as, for example, gender or racial or caste inequality are not. The ending of such inequalities therefore does not mean the end of capitalism. If by some miracle all the aims of feminist, anti-racist, anti-caste or ethnic, national and other such movements could be realised and all non-class oppressions got rid of, capitalism could still exist, society would still remain fundamentally divided on class lines. No doubt, the composition of the dominant class, and much else about the social order, would be different, but domination and subordination, based on class lines, would endure. Capitalism does not create inequalities of gender, race or caste – they have their autonomous causal mechanisms – and it does not normally need to permit them. They however persist in the capitalist social order because in subjecting all social relations to its requirements, capitalism also coopts, transforms and reinforces, inequalities or oppressions it did not create, and uses them in the interests of class exploitation. The important point is that these inequalities and oppressions – of gender, race, caste, etc. – are not in principle incompatible with capitalism. The disappearance of class inequalities on the other hand is by definition incompatible with capitalism. The abolition of class inequalities would by definition mean the end of capitalism. What is more, in contrast with the possible elimination of gender or racial or caste inequality which yet lets the class domination endure, the elimination of class inequality or exploitation would at least make possible the elimination of inequality based on gender, race, caste, etc. This is the necessary condition for the achievement of a social order in which these inequalities would eventually disappear. Of course, it is not a sufficient condition for this to happen. But it will open the door for an autonomous resolution of gender, racial, caste and other non-class oppressions as part of a project of full human emancipation.

Along with this basic inadequacy, to be particularly noticed is another in-built limitation of social movements flowing from 'civil society' as the concept underlying their theory and practice. 'Civil society' is by definition not only *not* the state, it also denotes privileging of the non-state. The concept not only masks the class nature of its components – multinational corporations, banks and mafia, set next to social movements, trade unions, civic bodies – it collectively demonises the state and posits the non-state as the authentic, democratic arena of struggle. The result is that social movements, and not only those which lack a political vocation for power, deliberately distance from the political arena and thus from any serious reflection on strategic issues. They remain at the sub-state level and therefore cannot point the way, either theoretically or practically, beyond the current neo-liberal globalist paradigm.

The idea of 'civil society' has been used by social movements (and NGOs and sundry other activist groups) to not only proclaim their indifference or opposition to the state, governments, parliaments and political parties but also reject them. What this means is well expressed in Emir Sader's critical observations on World Social Forum, a major, much-noticed 'civil society intervention' of recent years in which social movements, along with NGOs, have a dominant presence: 'The exclusive aspect of the emphasis on 'civil society' lies in its rejection of parties and governments, its embrace of the civil society/state opposition. This is more serious, not only because it means rejecting a potential weapon in a radically unequal contest but also, and more importantly, because the movement thus distances itself from the themes of power, the state, public sphere, political leadership and even, in a sense, from ideological struggle.... The result of this exclusion of parties and state, if pushed through, would severely limit the formulation of any alternatives to neoliberalism, confining such aspirations to a local or sectoral context – the NGOs' mantra, 'Think global, act local'; proposals for fair trade; 'ecologically sustainable development' – while giving up any attempts to build an alternative hegemony, or any global proposals to counter and defeat world capitalism's current neoliberal project.'

Social movements do not, and cannot, have an alternative hegemonic project, which would, by its nature, have to include states, governments and political parties as the means through which political and economic power is articulated in modern societies. They are unable to convert their not inconsiderable gains or advantages into political strength – whether at the level of governments and parliaments, or as mass mobilisations – that could effectively exercise a veto on the reigning neoliberal policies, or take other forms of political action. Their thinking here remains within the limits of the liberal critique of the state's actions and their activity, defined in opposition to the state, ends at the boundaries of liberal politics. And they themselves end up as more or less successful pressure groups within a political system dominated by the traditional politicians and parties.

The inadequacies we have pointed out do not take anything away from the importance and achievements of social movements and the associated identity struggles and voluntary activism said to be springing from 'civil society'. But this should not prevent us from seeing that this inadequacy not only has had a limiting effect on what they are able to achieve, it has also made them eminently adaptable and useful to the powers that be. They are not only easily accommodated by the established social order but have also come to serve and sustain it in various ways.

Most visible in the domain of voluntary activism are the 'civil society organisations' called 'Non-Governmental Organisations (NGOs)'. At a count in 1995, there were 29,000 of them operating internationally, some of them of multinational scale. Today there are at least 50,000 NGOs in third world countries, receiving more than ten billion dollars in funding from international financial institutions, European, U.S. and Japanese governmental agencies and local governments, their activities spanning a wide range of social sections – women, tribals, dalits, unorganised workers, fishermen, slum dwellers, etc. – and social concerns – in such areas as environment, human rights, education and culture, relief to people in situations of natural or social disasters, etc. A global phenomenon, they describe themselves as the vanguard of 'civil society' operating in the interstices of the 'global economy', speak of 'alternative development' at their conferences, even claim to represent a 'third way' between 'authoritarian statism' and 'savage market capitalism'. Distinctions having got blurred, much of the emancipatory rhetoric surrounding social movements has come to be harnessed to the NGOs. They have been seen as agents of progressive social change, capable of altering governmental policies, even resisting 'globalisation'. There *are* NGOs which have indeed striven to be such agents. Some have been deservedly described as 'militant' NGOs for their active opposition to specific anti-people policies and practices of governments – the U.S. government is known to have systematically attempted to coopt and thwart some of these NGOs, to replace their legitimate demands with its own corporate and imperial line. But even the best of NGOs cannot be seen as harbingers of 'alternative development' or as agencies of local or global civil society pitted against or resisting the established powers. As for most others: 'In many ways the hierarchical structures and the forms of transmission of "aid" and "training" resemble 19th century charity, and the promoters are not very different from Christian missionaries'. Another assessment goes even farther into the past: 'They can be compared to the Dominican and Franciscans of late feudal society, functioning as "the charitable campaigns and mendicant orders of Empire", playing a similar role in serving the people and sustaining the existing social order.'

It is significant that NGOs located in the advanced capitalist countries, the core zones of global capitalism, have overwhelmingly yet sought to implement their policies in the periphery or semi periphery, through their local agencies. To be particularly noticed, therefore, are the NGOs in the underdeveloped or 'developing' parts of the world, where they have mushroomed like anything in recent decades – in some parts of Indian state of Bihar, they say, one can even get a registered NGO as part of dowry! They have been more a 'rapidly expanding industry' than any kind of social movement.

Some are of course doing good, even admirable work among and for the people, but none of them can claim to be effective agencies of progressive social change. Most of them are bureaucratic structures catering to the particular interests and changing priorities of their funding agencies. They rely for their sustenance on private donations from individuals, foundations or big money houses who have motivations beyond just charity or 'do-gooding'. Though their voluntary and non-governmental character is emphasised, it is quite common for 'non-governmental' groups to rely substantially on official funding which again determines the interests to be pursued by them. In all cases serious social transformation is, obviously, no part of their agenda. It may be added that in looking after the interests of their funding agencies, NGOs have not been wanting in looking after their own interests – well-paid careers and relatively easy life, especially for the young who could have otherwise gone and done 'dangerous' things, and, for those at the top, the 'managers' and the 'bosses', there is the additional bonus of global jet-setting, what with the 'international conferencing' and 'marches' that are on all the time. Pointing out that 'the managers of the biggest NGOs manage million-dollar budgets and receive salaries and perks that are comparable to those of corporate CEOs', James Petras and Henry Veltmeyer have rather devastatingly observed: 'The NGOs worldwide have become the latest vehicle for upward mobility for the ambitious educated classes. Academics, journalists and professionals have abandoned earlier interests in poorly rewarded leftist movements for a lucrative career managing an NGO, bringing with them their organizational and rhetorical skills and a certain populist vocabulary. Today, thousands of NGO directors drive $40,000 four-wheel-drive sports utility vehicles from their fashionable suburban homes or apartments to their well-furnished offices and building complexes, leaving the children and domestic chores in the hands of servants and their yards to be tended by gardeners. They are more familiar with and spend more time at the overseas sites of their international conferences on poverty (Washington, Bangkok, Tokyo, Brussels, Rome, etc.) than the muddy villages of their own country. They are more adept at writing up new proposals to bring in hard currency for "deserving professionals" than risking a rap on the head from police attacking a demonstration of underpaid rural school teachers. NGO leaders are a new class not based on property ownership or government resources but derived from imperial funding and their own capacity to control significant popular groups. The NGO leaders can be conceived of as a kind of neo-comprador group that doesn't produce any useful commodity but does function to produce services for the donor countries, trading in domestic poverty for individual perks'. They add: 'The formal claims used by NGO directors to justify their positions – that they fight poverty, inequality, etc. – are self-serving and specious. There is a direct relation between the growth of NGOs and the decline of living standards: the proliferation of NGOs has not reduced structural unemployment or massive displacements of peasants, nor provided livable wage levels for the growing army of informal workers. What NGOs have done is provide a thin stratum of professionals with income in hard currency who are able to escape the ravages of the neoliberal economy that affects their country and people and to climb within the existing social class structure.' In India it is not only cynics who have pointed out how commercial ethics has taken over the NGOs and their networking, how poverty mongering has became a lucrative business and poverty alleviation has enriched many, how the 'activist industry' blooms whenever a disaster overtakes the people...

Most significant is the way NGOs are being neutralised and coopted into the global capitalist system through its international conferencing, increased funding from abroad, including from international financial institutions and, above all, through partnership in the international business of 'development'. 'For the last decade', a World Bank president has recently told us, 'we have held an active dialogue with the organisations of civil society, including through the projects that we are financing'. Distinguishing between 'unreasonable' NGOs and 'reasonable' NGOs (those willing to 'implement' its policies), the Bank has sought to use them to legitimise itself and acquire a 'human face' for its inhuman structural adjustment programmes. With the state forced to retreat from social welfare, the NGOs have been championed as an alternative to the state in matters of education, health care etc., to the benefit of the local and global structures of capitalist power and production. The *Economist* has noted: 'The IMF, long regarded as impermeable to outsiders, now runs seminars to teach NGOs the nuts and bolts of country-programme design, so that they can better monitor what the Fund is doing and (presumably) understand the rationale for the Fund's loan conditions. Horst Kohler, the IMF's new boss, has been courting NGOs. Jim Wolfensohn, the Bank's boss, has long fawned in their direction, but in the Bank too the pace of bowing down has been stepped up.... Mark Malloch Brown, the administrator of the United Nations Development Programme, has gone further. He has a board of NGOs (including some fairly radical ones) to advise him...'

The sharpest critical assessment here has come from James Petras and Henry Veltmeyer who, in a detailed study of the functioning and role of the NGOs in the Third World, particularly in Latin America, have seen them to be directly serving the interests of imperialism and domestic reactionary regimes. Their argument is best conveyed by quoting a few passages: 'As opposition to neoliberalism grew in the early 1980s, the U.S. and European governments and the World Bank increased their funding of NGOs. There is a direct relation between the growth of social movements challenging the neoliberal model and the effort to subvert them by creating alternative forms of social action through the NGOs. The basic point of convergence between the NGOs and the World Bank was their common opposition to "statism". On the surface the NGOs criticized the state from a "left" perspective defending civil society, while the right did so in the name of the market. In reality, however, the World Bank, the neoliberal regimes, and western foundations co-opted and encouraged the NGOs to undermine the national welfare state by providing social services to compensate the victims of the multinational corporations (MNCs). In other words, as the neoliberal regimes at the top devastated communities by inundating the country with cheap imports, extracting external debt payment, abolishing labor legislation, and creating a growing mass of low-paid and unemployed workers, the NGOs were funded to provide "self-help" projects, "popular education", and job training, to temporarily absorb small groups of poor, to co-opt local leaders, and to undermine anti-system struggles.'

'In reality NGOs are not "non-governmental" organizations. They receive funds from overseas governments, work as private subcontractors for local governments and/or are subsidized by corporate-funded private foundations with close working relations with the state. Frequently they openly collaborate with governmental agencies at home or overseas. Their programs are not accountable to local people but to overseas donors who "review" and "oversee" the performance of the NGOs according to their own criteria and interests. NGO officials are self-appointed and one of their key tasks is to design proposals that will secure funding. In many cases this requires NGO leaders to find out the issues that most interest Western funding elites and to shape proposals accordingly.'

'Today most Left movements and popular spokespeople focus their criticism on the IMF, the World Bank, multinational corporations, private banks, etc., who fix the macroeconomic agenda for the pillage of the Third World. This is an important task. However, the assault on the industrial base, independence and living standards of the Third World takes place on both the macroeconomic and micro-socio-political levels. The egregious effects of structural adjustment policies on waged and salaried workers, peasants and small national business people generate potential national popular discontent. And that is where the NGOs come into the picture; to mystify and deflect that discontent away from direct attacks on corporate/banking power structures and profits and towards local micro-projects, apolitical "grass roots" self-exploitation and "popular education" that avoids class analysis of imperialism and capitalist profit-taking.'

'NGOs emphasize projects, not movements. They

"mobilize" people to produce at the margins, not to struggle to control the basic means of production and wealth. They focus on the technical and financial assistance aspects of projects, not on structural conditions that shape the everyday lives of people. The NGOs co-opt the language of the Left – "Popular power," "Empowerment," "gender equality," "sustainable development," "bottom-up leadership," etc. The problem is that this language is linked to a framework of collaboration with donors and government agencies committed to non-confrontational politics. The local nature of NGO activity means that "empowerment" never goes beyond influencing small areas of social life with limited resources, always within conditions permitted by the neoliberal state and macro economy.... The NGOs fragment poor communities into sectoral and subsectoral groupings unable to see the larger social picture that afflicts them and even less able to unite in struggle against the system.'

'The structure and nature of NGOs, with their "apolitical" posture and their focus on self-help, depoliticize and demobilize the poor. They reinforce the electoral processes encouraged by the neoliberal parties and mass media. Political education about the nature of imperialism, the class basis of neoliberalism and the class struggle between exporters and temporary workers are avoided. Instead the NGOs discuss "the excluded," the "powerless," "extreme poverty" and "gender and racial discrimination," without moving beyond the superficial symptoms to engage the social system that has produced these conditions. Incorporating the poor into the neoliberal economy through purely "private voluntary action," the NGOs create a political world where the appearance of solidarity and social action cloaks a conservative conformity with the international and national power structure.'

'Contrary to the NGOers' image of themselves as innovative grass roots leaders, they are in reality grass roots reactionaries who complement the work of the IMF by pushing privatization "from below" and demobilizing popular movements, thus undermining resistance.... The role of the NGOs in the micro projects is to neutralize political opposition at the bottom while neoliberalism is promoted at the top.... The emphasis on "local activity" serves the neoliberal regimes since it allows its foreign and domestic backers to dominate macro-socio-economic policy.'

To be particularly noted is this criticism: 'The NGO ideology, of "private voluntaristic activity," undermines the sense of the "public": the idea that the government has an obligation to look after its citizens and provide them with life, liberty, and the pursuit of happiness, that the political responsibility of the state is essential for the wellbeing of citizens. Against this notion of public responsibility, the NGOs foster the neoliberal idea of private responsibility for social problems and the importance of private resources to solve these problems. In effect they impose a double burden on the poor who continue to pay taxes to finance the neoliberal state to serve the rich, but are left with private self-exploitation to take care of their own needs'; and: 'Typically, NGO ideologues counterpose "state" power to "local" power. State power is, they argue, distant from its citizens, autonomous and arbitrary, and it tends to develop interests different from and opposed to those of its citizens, while local power is necessarily closer and more responsive to the people. But apart from historical cases where the reverse has also been true, this leaves out the essential relation between state and local power – the simple truth that state power wielded by a dominant, exploiting class will undermine progressive local initiatives, while that same power in the hands of progressive forces can reinforce such initiatives.'

Petras-Veltmeyer critique is eminently valid, though, as we have already noted, it does not apply to every single NGO. Petras and Veltmeyer themselves recognise 'that there are a great many different types of NGOs and that many do criticize and organize against adjustment policies, the IMF, debt payments, etc. and that it is unfair to lump them all in the same bag.' And, as Petras has elsewhere written: 'While the mass of NGOs are increasingly instruments of neoliberalism, there is a small minority which attempt to develop an alternative strategy that is supportive of anti-imperialist and class politics. None of them receive funds from the World Bank, European, or U.S.

governmental agencies. They support efforts to link local power to struggles for state power. They link local projects to national socio-political movements: occupying large landed estates, defending public property and national ownership against multinationals. They provide political solidarity to social movements involved in struggles to expropriate land. They support women's struggles linked to class perspectives. They recognize the importance of politics in defining local and immediate struggles. They believe that local organizations should fight at the national level and that national leaders must be accountable to local activists.' Even so the fact remains that, notwithstanding this 'small minority' of NGOs and whatever be the subjective motivations of those involved, much local, grass roots, popular activity has come to be structured and appropriated by the ruling classes through the NGOs. As intermediaries between the ruling elites above and the people below, NGOs have served to effectively depoliticise the latter in the name of working for them. Imparting a pluralistic character to the on-going 'development', NGOs have not only masked its monotonic reality as capitalist development but also helped rein in and depoliticise popular opposition to it. With the NGO's focus on management of life at ground level, major struggles over fundamental choices in economy or politics are, much in the manner of post-modernists, ruled out. The rhetoric over 'empowerment of people' conceals the fact that, as with social movements and 'civil society activism' in general, the state as the site of struggle stands abandoned and with it stands abandoned the struggle for political power which, obfuscations of bourgeois political theory notwithstanding, remains the pre-eminent form of power in society. NGOs have served to delegitimise people-oriented politics and people's struggle for power in the state.

'Identity politics' is another recent phenomenon, seen to be springing from civil society, or otherwise, that needs to be taken note of. This politics, thought and action on the terrain of 'identity' (gender, ethnicity, race or caste, nationality etc.), while sharing in quite a few of the inadequacies of social movements and NGOs, has in-built limitations of its own. For all the hype over it, 'identity politics' has almost invariably served interests other than it is supposed to promote. The best of identity struggles are a necessary development – rather a stage of development – for the long disadvantaged and discriminated against, often lower status people now 'awakening to life and politics'. They have focussed attention on and contested the long established or imposed oppressions and subordinations which have to be dismantled before any society can rightfully call itself democratic. They have won important civil and political rights for their people, lessened their oppression somewhat, brought them some respect and dignity among fellow human beings. But they can hardly claim to have significantly advanced the interests of the people concerned or the cause of radical change in society. Instead most of them have advanced the interests of the elites within and served as adjuncts to ruling class politics outside.

There is much to be said for 'identity' as a form of community, for the sense of belonging its gives to its members, the social, cultural and psychological support it provides, especially in times of personal or social distress. But 'identity' *as such* is not something good or sacred, a value in itself. Historically constituted and not pre-given, it carries a whole lot of history's burdensome baggage, mud of the times as it were, much within it that limits and diminishes human beings – its own injustices, discriminations and denial of rights, hierarchies, inequalities and class cleavages, superstitions and otherwise oppressive social practices, and almost invariably a vision which is a barrier to seeing things the way they really are. There is a glaring disjunction between this reality and the emancipatory rhetoric of the proponents of 'identity politics'.

Not pre-given, 'identity' is also not frozen or exclusive at a particular point of time. There is always an overlap of identities. Identity politics too often isolates and fetishises only one dimension of the inescapable complexity of every human being. It blinds its members to their commonalities – in terms of basic needs and interests – with the vast majority of their fellow human beings. This not only undermines their own struggle but also makes them vulnerable to the divisive politics of the ruling classes above and the elites within. 'Identity consciousness' is in many ways a much corrupted consciousness, a hindrance in the way of developing consciousness for collective action which *all* sections of oppressed and exploited people need in their struggle for a better life.

The variety of identity politics, it should be remembered, also includes what has been described as 'hate-filled identity politics' where the dominant elites stop at nothing in fomenting and manipulating divisions among people to advance their own interests, and the dangerous fundamentalist (or communal) movements based on religious identities. The latter come up and survive, even thrive on the social material basis provided by failed or frustrated socio-economic development – but as symptoms and not solutions of the crisis in society, really important only in relation to the problems they raise or confront. *Jehadis* in Pakistan and elsewhere is one example. *Hindutava* in India is another. Fundamentalist Islam may be viewed as a metaphor for third world revolt against western capitalist decadence and domination, but it has no answers to the problems of the people – vast masses of the poor in the so-called Islamic countries – seeking a better human existence for themselves. Hindutava in India can only perpetuate fratricidal conflict and provide ideological basis for right-wing neo-fascist politics.

It has been suggested that even the best of identity politics is a project only for a particular section of society when what is needed is a universalist project, one for *all* human beings. Hence the plea for uniting the best of identity politics with the universalistic legacy of socialism. This however is not a matter of somehow adding up the two. What is really required is a transformation of identity politics. A more meaningful, truly purposeful, proposition would be that even the best of identity struggles cannot realise their aims except as part of a struggle for socialism. The oppressed identities, in particular, need to recognise the reality of class differences and the centrality of the class question. As Petras and Veltmeyer, commenting on identity politics of the feminist NGOs, have written: 'Take, for example, the Chilean or Indian feminist living in a plush suburb and drawing a salary fifteen to twenty times that of her domestic servant who works six days a week. Class differences within gender determine housing, living standards, health, educational opportunities and who appropriates surplus value. Yet the great majority of NGOs operate on the basis of identity politics and argue that this is the basic point of departure for the new, post-modern politics. Identity politics does not challenge the male dominated elite world of IMF privatization, multinational corporations and local landlords. Rather, it focuses on "patriarchy" in the household, family violence, divorce, family planning, etc. In other words, it fights for gender equality within the micro-world of exploited peoples in which the exploited and impoverished male worker or peasant emerges as the main villain. While no one should support gender exploitation or discrimination at any level, the feminist NGOs do a gross disservice to working women by subordinating them to the greater exploitation of sweatshops which benefit upper-class men and women, rent-collecting male and female landlords, and CEOs of both sexes. The reason the feminist NGOs ignore the "big picture" and focus on local issues and personal politics is because billions of dollars flow annually in that direction. If feminist NGOs began to engage in land occupations with men and women landless workers in Brazil, Indonesia, Thailand or the Philippines, or if they joined in general strikes of mainly female low-paid rural school teachers against structural adjustment policies, the NGO spigot would be turned off by their imperial donors. Better to beat up the local patriarch scratching out an existence in an isolated village in Luzon.' In other words, the oppressed identities need to recognize that class is the site of the structural oppression that conditions and mediates all other and that its abolition alone opens the possibility of ending their own oppressions and ensuring the development of their distinctive personalities in a democratic socialist society, and also that as class, the oppressed of each identity have an objective, material basis to join with the oppressed of other identities in a struggle to achieve this. Hence the necessity of articulating their struggles with class struggle.

Otherwise they are likely to degenerate into an 'identitarianism' which will divide the oppressed even more, distort and corrupt their consciousness still further, and end up serving the interests not of the common people but of the exploiting and other elite elements within who are only too eager to find a place for themselves in the economy and politics of the oppressive system. The system on its part has never been averse to accommodating them.

Frances Fox Piven has written: 'If identity politics is ubiquitous because of what it offers people in protection, comfort and pride, it has also been a bane upon humankind, the source of unending tragedy. The fatal flaw in identity politics is easily recognized. Class politics, at least in principle, promotes vertical cleavages, mobilising people around axes which broadly correspond to hierarchies of power, and which promote challenges to these hierarchies. By contrast, identity politics fosters lateral cleavages which are unlikely to reflect fundamental conflicts over societal power and resources and, indeed, may seal popular allegiance to the ruling classes that exploit them. This fatal flaw at the very heart of a popular politics based on identity is in turn regularly exploited by elites... the vulnerability to manipulation resulting from identity politics is as characteristic of modern societies as tribal societies.'

She goes on: '... identity politics makes people susceptible to the appeals of modern nationalism, to the bloody idea of loyalty to state and flag, which is surely one of the more murderous ideas to beset humankind. State builders cultivate a sort of race pride to build allegiance to an abstract state, drawing on the ordinary and human attachments that people form to their group and their locality, and drawing also on the animosity to the Other that is typically the complement of these attachments.' Nationalism, I may add, is not always or necessarily the unqualified good it is not unoften made out to be, especially in the post-colonial countries where people had fought for their freedom under the banner of nationalism. It is not always the legitimate nationalism of oppressed nations or nationalities under alien domination, or of national liberation struggles. Far more often it is the ideological tool of ruling class politics which does not hesitate to sacrifice people to the 'nation' in the interests of the rich and powerful. With the ruling classes, in the normal pursuit of their interests or when faced with situations of crisis in the polity, nationalism in our time has often taken all sorts of anti-people, statist or racist, or fascist or imperialist forms, providing ideological support or cover to the emergence of reactionary authoritarian regimes.

I would conclude this discussion by returning to the question of social movements which remain among the more significant progressive developments of recent decades. These movements have registered important gains for the people. But even where they are strongest, say the feminists in the United States or the Greens in Germany, their gains do not add up to much. Women in the poorer sections have seen no improvement in their condition in the U.S., and Germany, with the Green party a partner in government, has witnessed no shift towards an eco-friendly social order or a shift in its subservience to America's global politics which is visibly most destructive of environment today. And in both places, as with social movements elsewhere, they have adapted themselves to, if not actually propped up, the established structures of power. Social movements have opened no paths to greater justice, equality or emancipation anywhere. Their stress on 'difference', 'identity' and 'pluralism' easily collapses back into liberalism. In place of any effort to develop a general movement directed at transforming the roots of society's contemporary malaise, we have a proliferation of separate 'movements' each of which, at best, acknowledges the moral right of the other to stake out its own ground. As single issue movements, with moralism substituted for analysis and without any coherent and comprehensive alternative to the existing system, they stand marginalised and stagnant, accommodated in the system either as a species of social democracy, not too different from the classic variety, although with more rhetoric about ecology, sexism, racism, etc. or as confined to middle class ghettoes in which many current movements have trapped themselves. The system has little trouble accommodating *bourgeois* feminism, anti-racism or civil rights, sexual liberation or environmentalism, that is, any of the social movements so long as they do not threaten the system, its overall exploitative logic or capital accumulation process – an accommodation which in turn legitimises and sustains the system. An interesting device here, typical of our globalised times, has been international conferencing over issues posed by the social movements – 'summit-led humanitarianism' which in its own way helps legitimise and sustain an essentially inhumane system.

Their accommodation in the system draws our attention to what is, in a historical perspective, possibly the most important aspect of the social movements. A long time back, James Connolly, the famous Irish revolutionary had said: 'When questions of "class interests" are eliminated from public controversy a victory is thereby gained for the possessing, conservative class, whose only hope of security lies in such elimination. Like a fraudulent trustee, the bourgeois dreads nothing so much as an impartial and rigid inquiry into the validity of his title deeds. Hence the bourgeois press and politicians incessantly strive to inflame the working class mind to fever heat upon questions outside the range of their own class interests.' Social movements have been very much a part of this class struggle from above which is always on in capitalist society.

Bourgeois politics early recognised that such movements have tended to rely on the extent to which they can *avoid* specifically implicating the capitalist order and its class system, never posing any kind of threat to the larger and more potent structures of exploitation, oppression and organisation that capitalism is, whatever its historically specific forms. Their anchoring of politics away from class struggle into non-class or cross-class contradictions was welcomed. Social movements (and the associated 'identity politics) were counterposed to class politics and sought to be manipulated to the benefit of bourgeois politics. Their 'autonomy' and 'non-party', even 'non-political' character was emphasised and promoted to keep them away from radical or revolutionary Left, which however did not prevent their being invited to participate in bourgeois politics of an ill-defined 'struggle for democracy' or 'good globalisation' or, more recently, 'another world is possible'. More than anything else, these movements were furnished with a conceptual framework, 'civil society', which, as we have seen, has the dubious merit of making invisible the reality of power relations which constitute capitalism, the dominant structure of coercion which reaches into every corner of our lives, public and private. Here we can do no better than quote Ellen Meiksins Wood again:

> But even if we stop short of openly embracing capitalism, we can simply evade the issue. That is the effect of all-purpose concepts like 'identity' or 'civil society' as they are currently used. The capitalist system, its totalizing unity, can be conceptualized away by adopting loose conceptions of civil society or by submerging class in catch-all categories like 'identity' and by disaggregating the social world into particular and separate realities. The social relations of capitalism can be dissolved into an unstructured and fragmented plurality of identities and differences. Questions about historical causality or political efficacy can be side-stepped, and there is no need to ask how various identities are situated in the prevailing social structure because the existence of the social structure can be denied altogether.
>
> In a sense, the concept of 'identity' has simply replaced the 'interest groups' of pluralist theories in conventional political science, whose object was to deny the importance of class in capitalist democracies. According to both the old and the new pluralisms, 'interest groups' or 'identities' are separate but equal, or at least equivalent, *plural* rather than *different*. And our democracy is a kind of market-place where these interests or identities meet and compete, though they may come together in loose alliances or political parties. Both pluralisms, of course, have the effect of denying the systemic unity of capitalism, or its very existence as a social system; and both insist on the heterogeneity of capitalist society, while losing sight of its increasingly global power of homogenization...
>
> What is alarming about these theoretical developments is not that they violate some doctrinaire Marxist prejudice concerning the privileged status of class. Of course, the whole object of the exercise is to side-line class, to dissolve it in all-embracing categories which deny it any privileged status, or even any political relevance at all. But that is not the real problem. The problem is

that theories which do not differentiate – and, yes, 'privilege', if that means ascribing causal or explanatory priorities – among various social institutions and 'identities' cannot deal critically with capitalism at all. The consequence of these procedures is to sweep the whole question under the rug. And whither capitalism, so goes the socialist idea. Socialism is the specific alternative to capitalism. Without capitalism, we have no need of socialism; we can make do with very diffuse and indeterminate concepts of democracy which are not specifically opposed to any identifiable system of social relations, in fact do not even recognize any such system. What we are left with then is a fragmented plurality of oppressions and a fragmented plurality of emancipatory struggles. Here is another irony: what claims to be a more universalistic project than traditional socialism is actually less so. Instead of the universalist project of socialism and the integrative politics of the struggle against class exploitation, we have a plurality of essentially disconnected particular struggles...

The replacement of socialism by an indeterminate concept of democracy, or the dilution of diverse and different social relations into catch-all categories like 'identity' or 'difference', or loose conceptions of 'civil society', represent a surrender to capitalism and its ideological mystifications. By all means let us have diversity, difference, and pluralism; but not this kind of *undifferentiated* and unstructured pluralism. What we need is a pluralism which does indeed acknowledge diversity and difference – and that means not just *plurality* or *multiplicity*. It means a pluralism which also recognizes historical realities, which does not deny the systemic unity of capitalism, which can tell the difference between the constitutive relations of capitalism and *other* inequalities and oppressions with *different* relations to capitalism, a *different* place in the systemic logic of capitalism, and therefore a different role in our struggles against it. The socialist project should be *enriched* by the resources and insights of the new social movements, not impoverished by resorting to them as an excuse for disintegrating the struggle against capitalism. We should not confuse respect for the plurality of human experience and social struggles with a complete dissolution of historical causality, where there is nothing *but* diversity, difference, and contingency, no unifying structures, no logic of process, no capitalism and therefore no negation of it, no universal project of human emancipation...

Whatever be their achievements or potential for radical change, the long-term future of the (now not so new) 'new social movements' remains uncertain. It is difficult to say whether these movements at the centre or the periphery are capable of making headway against the objective challenge facing them, recognising capitalism as the real enemy and moving against it or be eventually wholly absorbed by it, or even otherwise wither away in the current crisis of capitalism. We can certainly be hopeful that the best of these movements would yet find their way, sooner rather than later, to a radical, if not revolutionary politics of basic transformations in society. But as they now exist, their coherence or potential must not be overrated, whatever high visibility they may have at national or international seminars or conferences, or in the media. Their gains have been much too fragmentary and partial. Even the stronger or more significant of these movements – ecologism, feminism, pacifism, etc. – have not been able, in any stable or significant measure, to produce a new culture or organisations that will unite with broad masses of workers, peasants and marginal layers of society for a radical social change. A base which is too narrow and fractured, a consciousness which in the very nature of things is limiting of vision and action, a practice which is most flawed theoretically, they have – when not by choice apolitical or anti-political – failed to provide an effective alternative politics to that of the dominant bourgeois formations, much less project the vision of a different, better social order. They have, by choice or default, invariably rejected a materialist understanding and class-structural view of social reality they have sought to change, and almost all of them have been either negated or accommodated within the interests of capital or are otherwise stagnating, and *as such* – but only *as such* – can even be described as failed social movements.

It is not that social movements are not surviving or continuing to struggle. But without class and a materialist analysis at the core of their struggles they remain isolated and limited in their ability to achieve their ends, since the real structures of power remain untouched and unchanged. In the U.S., for example, we have had strongest of the feminist movements in the west and the much celebrated Black civil rights movement, addressing two most vital issues in American society. The majority of women do the lowest paid work in the United States (as they do elsewhere too) and feminisation of manual work in core capitalist countries is part of the strategic offensive of capital against labour as such. Besides, women's unpaid housework is a fundamental component in minimising the aggregate wage bill, hence important for ensuring a certain rate of profit. And the majority of blacks constitute a distinct underclass in the U.S. economy that has been reproduced over and over again since the time of slavery. Despite all the celebrated successes of feminism in certain areas of academic and cultural life in the United States, the situation of the majority that is the poor women has shown no improvement. And despite all the hype over the achievements of the 'Gandhian' civil rights movement, the black youth have remained the underclass they were. The issue of justice to this vast majority of women and men goes to the very heart of the *totality* of U.S. life and cannot be really resolved without structural, that is revolutionary transformations. It is this understanding of social reality which has all along eluded the theory and practice of the social movements.

It is significant and worth pointing out that the main lesson that grew out of the later phase of the black civil rights movement was that a poor people's movement which is to continue to advance must eventually evolve from a question of rights to a question of power, from civil or political to human emancipation. And this requires a shift in the nature of the organised struggle towards class politics, that is, collective resistance to capitalism. It is not surprising that by 1968, shortly before his assassination, Martin Luther King Jr. was publicly speaking of what he called 'radical redistribution of economic and political power' and 'a radical reconstruction of American society', of 'self-transforming and structure-transforming direct action'. 'We are engaged in the class struggle', he publicly stated, and pointed out: 'We have been in a reform movement... But after Selma and the voting rights bill (in 1965) we moved into a new era which must be an era of revolution. I think we must see the great distinction here between a reform movement and a revolutionary movement'. The lesson here is relevant for all social movements as people's movements.

The moral force of the new social movements as a whole is unquestionable but the choice facing them is equally clear. The autonomy they claim and the qualities that give them their strength also account for their weakness, because this prevents them from looking around and seeing that the fulfilment of their own ends or emancipatory needs lies in the overcoming of capitalism and not reform within it. It makes them resistant to their transformation into agents of a fundamental change. 'Popular' identity and unity is retained at the cost of their capacity to act as a force for social transformation. They can become such a force, substantially effective even in achieving their own specific ends, only by recognising the structural imperatives in social relations and domination and therefore harnessing their popular power to the politics of class which aims at transformation of the existing social order and class relations. In other words, these social movements may be 'new' but their power to reshape society is critically dependent on the extent to which they can connect their struggles to those of the 'old' social movements, the class-based movements of workers, poor peasants and the landless and other exploited classes – albeit in ways that will radically transform the latter, *their* practice of class politics.

It may be added that a class-ward shift would also enable 'civil society activism' associated with new social movements to overcome some of its major dilemmas by providing it with a much needed framework of reference for understanding the world and the place of their 'activism' in it. It would help this activism to better use its resources of people's traditional wisdom, immediate experience and common discourse for mobilisational and organisational purposes by backing them with an insightful systemic analysis. Its politics of local governance, voluntary association and community empowerment will become more effective as programmes informed by class content tie it to larger questions of restructuring the polity at state and local levels. It will also open up the possibility of broader alliances to face up to the opposition and hostility of the locally entrenched power structures and the inevitable confrontations with the state.

That 'new' social movements need to connect with and transform the class politics of 'old' social movements also sets a parallel task for the latter. Marxism and Marxist-led movements have to face up to the organisational and strategic challenges posed by this expansion of radical democratic movements beyond the bounds of the traditional workers and peasants movements. The primary need here is to move away from 'economism' which has plagued them for long decades now, persuading them to focus on narrowly conceived, economic class contradictions only and limiting the struggle at only this level, to the neglect of other contradictions over issues which the new social movements have now emphasized, and thus failing to challenge capitalism as a whole system, in every aspect of our lives. Unfortunately this 'economism' still persists in the movement so that even when the importance of these other contradictions (and new needs) is seen, it is not understood that, autonomous though far from being entirely autonomous phenomena, these contradictions are deeply rooted in the existing structures and values of the capitalist mode of production, and that, generating a challenge to the system at several other, non-economic levels, they are setting forth anew, in their own way, the problem of overcoming the system, while at the same time providing, in their ensemble, yet another basis – the subjects and movements – for doing so,.

What the situation demands is a great renewal of theory and practice of Marxism, a new discourse of struggle without which the old movements will remain mired in economism and the new movements mere expressions of anguish or distress. At the theoretical level, Marxism's critical analysis of capitalism, avoiding both broad or abstract statements and economistic kind of class analysis of recent decades, must be expanded to deal with such issues as ecology and feminism – which have had only secondary importance so far, even treated as distraction from the 'real' struggle or as issues best left to be addressed 'after the revolution'. It has to accord them and other less-exclusively class-functional or class-centred issues a central, non-reductive importance, and be specific and concrete in establishing their linkages with the structural logic of capitalism as a systemic whole. A proper Marxist understanding must recognise capitalism as a total system of exploitation which has invented or adapted many kinds of oppression and destructive practices and whose commodity relation and its spin-offs have vitally permeated all aspects of our lives. At the practical level, the movement has to recognise the pervasiveness of the capitalist system and view the struggles against its separate evils as part of the struggle for human liberation and therefore as complementary. It must challenge capitalism wherever it produces misery and oppression, thwarts human creativity, threatens our existence and debases our world.

It was never the Marxist position that all struggles must be subsumed within organised forms of the class. Even if not adequately addressed, the issues and concerns that new social movements have put on the political agenda – women's rights, anti-sexism, anti-racism, ecology, peace, rights of oppressed nations or nationalities or of other oppressed sections within societies – have been part of the socialist agenda since the days of Marx; and there are many people in the 'new social movements' who are themselves Marxists or socialists and who conceive their concerns as bound up with socialism. The need today is to recover and enhance this agenda by a fruitful exchange and cooperation with the new movements that have come up on these issues and to gather and organise those who are now dispersed in these movements, the 'submerged left' as it has been, in view of its radical potential, called.

This does not mean abandoning class politics but rather moving from economistic and class-reductionist to a genuinely Marxist practice of class politics. Many things which the old generation of revolutionaries including communists did not do, or did badly, or have stopped doing have still to be done by those who, coming after them, would develop a people's movement for a revolutionary transformation of society. And a genuinely Marxist class politics is one of these.

Only such a renewal of Marxist theory and practice can help

make the struggle against the currently hegemonic capitalism more pervasive and ultimately also more effective.

XVI

A people's movement for socialist transformation of society, if it is to continue to advance must evolve from its particular or general concerns to the question of power in the state. This is not to suggest any immediate seizure of the Winter Palace or starting of an armed struggle to capture power. What is posited is that the working people's movement as it advances from below must aim at ultimately winning state power - however distant this winning at a particular point of time might be. For socialist politics issues of state and class power are always at the centre of things, and the ultimate aim remains winning power in the state without which no socialist transformation is possible. Though unevenly theorised, or theorised mostly in relation to specific situations, the tradition of revolutionary Marxism can yet provide needful guidance in this regard, helping us find answers to old unresolved problems and problems that have come up in recent times. The subject has been touched upon in different contexts earlier. Here I would like to make a few additional observations on three crucially important , inter-related issues; state and political power, democracy and revolutionary politics, and the question of political party.

For socialism to become viable as an emancipatory project, working people's power in the state is, as just suggested, a necessary condition. Of course there is the prior and continuing need for the socialist forces to acquire a certain degree of hegemony and social power in society which can ensure effective popular sanctions for their control over the state. But political or state power remains the cutting edge of a socialist transformation. Lenin was right in pointing out that 'the key question of every revolution is undoubtedly the question of state power. What class holds power decides everything... The question of power cannot be evaded or brushed aside, because it is the key question determining everything in a revolution's development, and in its foreign and domestic politics'. It is impossible for socialists to set out on the road to socialism unless or until state power is transferred from the ruling capitalist classes to the working classes, that is, political power is *really* in the hands of the working people and the state, really a transformed state, is available to them for their own purpose of a socialist transformation of society.

Marxist view of the class nature of the state remains valid and this holds true for bourgeois democracy too, which is only another historical form of state as a class system of power. But it is not adequate to describe the state, as important sections of the Left traditionally do, primarily in terms of 'an instrument' or 'an organ' – this, at best, grasps only one, albeit an important, aspect of the modern state. We need to recognise the obviously *non-monolithic nature*, on the one hand, of class domination where, almost invariably, what we have is an alliance or a coalition of ruling classes with real, even if non-antagonistic, internal conflict of interests, and on the other, of the material and ideological structures of the modern state that are today far too many and massively diverse, and scattered all over vertically and horizontally – which, incidentally, makes the state itself a possible 'arena of class struggle'. The metaphor of 'instrument' or 'organ', being very partial, can be quite misleading. It fails, for example, to make sense of the role of Louis Bonaparte in France, or Bismarck in Germany, or the Czarist state in Russia. Strictly speaking, in none of these cases can the state be regarded as an 'organ' of the capitalist class even though each one of them more or less actively facilitated the development of capitalism in their respective countries. The metaphor 'organ' also obscures the important possibility of state's relative autonomy from any given ruling class or classes, which the state often, if not always, needs to have precisely in order to manage and promote *the common interests* of the ruling classes *as a whole*. The state, however, is never autonomous from these interests, from the socio-economic exploitative structure of a class-divided society which it essentially serves.

This is not to deny that different structures of the state, its institutions and apparatuses, at a particular point of time may be in the hands of a particular fragment of ruling class or classes, who may use them to promote particular interests or even settle intra- or inter-class quarrels or conflicts. But a proper Marxist view of the state must see it as the organiser of society in the interests of the class-exploitative structure taken as a whole – and this includes, as Gramsci put it, 'the entire complex of practical and theoretical activities with which the ruling class not only justifies and maintains its dominance, but manages to win the active consent of those over whom it rules.'

However within this more adequate Marxian view of the state, the traditional emphasis on the class character of 'the state apparatus' and the need to transform it for purposes of a socialist transition retains its importance. The principle involved in Marx's famous statement that 'the working class cannot simply lay hold of the ready-made state machinery and wield it for its own purposes' and Lenin's interpretation that 'Marx's idea is that the working class must break up, smash the "ready-made state machinery," and not confine itself merely to laying hold of it', remain as valid as ever. The real point here is not to interpret 'break up' or 'smash' literally, but to recognise that in one way or another the bourgeois state apparatus, which has been fashioned and long used as an instrument of bourgeois rule, must be effectively and definitively transformed into an instrument of *anti*-bourgeois rule. The changes required will of course vary according to particular historical circumstances. But as historical experience has made it abundantly clear, it is not enough that leading positions in the government come to be occupied by representatives of the working people. What is needed is far-reaching changes in the structure and personnel of the government involving the organisation of executive, legislative and judicial systems, staffing of the police and armed forces, overhaul of elite-oriented educational system, etc., so that the state apparatus is a loyal and reliable instrument in the hands of the representatives of the masses. This is a need which Laski constantly urged upon the Labour Party in England when it still had some pretensions to socialism. 'We have to invent another kind of State' is how Pierre Bourdieu, the eminent sociologist recently put it.

In this regard it is important to note that historical experience has fully vindicated the Marxian analysis of class character of the modern state. We need not, at the moment, go back to classic cases, like that of Chile for example, or to the well-documented writings of Miliband and other scholars. In the more recent period in the West, it has been manifest in the confrontational position the state has adopted against the working class and the trade unions – from Reagan's smashing of the air controllers' strike to Thatcher's police-state savaging of the miners' unions, to Gonzalez's and Jospin's efforts to break the general strikes in their countries – and the continued dismantling of the welfare state. This class character is today equally visible in the 'national' states of the post-colonial third world. Acting as 'the executor of the economic necessities of the national situation' – as Engels once phrased it – even the better among them, while they have secured a degree of third-worldist capitalist development, have failed to deliver the promised equity and distributive justice to the common people. They have however not failed to serve as instruments of coercion and repression against them. The ruling elites' well-known corruption, their use of 'state as private property' and any kind of power in the state as a means of 'rapid private accumulation', only underline the essential class character of the post-colonial state, making it all the more a part of the problem than any kind of solution in post-colonial societies.

Both in the West and elsewhere in the third world, the state has been and continues to be a class state. All those who seek a genuine radical or revolutionary transformation of society, including the best of those involved in 'grass roots' activism, or 'new social movements' will do well to recognise the harsh fact – the class nature and power of the state. At the very least, those who would leave the state alone, as a certain kind of radicalism advocates, need to know that the state will not leave *them* alone.

This kind of radicalism decries the so-called 'big politics' of the state and leaves it for 'politics of the small', of the 'grass roots' movements, it devalues and denies the role of the state in favour of the 'new instrumentalities' of voluntary activism or 'non-party political formations'. This not only means an abandonment of the most important terrain of struggle against the system which well serves the interests of the powers that be, but also betrays an abysmal ignorance of the requirements of any radical reconstruction of society. Much as we must value *all* instrumentalities of people's social power from below, the role of the state still remains decisive here. As the Marxist view has it, while the state must ultimately disappear, people in the meantime need the state, a state of their own, to eliminate classes and inequalities, to help them build a just and humane social order. The perspective here is thus sketched by Ralph Miliband: 'The power of the dominant class and its allies can be overcome; but overcoming it requires an effective state. To say this is not statist, elitist, undemocratic, male chauvinist ('the state is male'), or to be unaware of the dangers the labels point to. But the way to obviate these dangers is not to devalue and deny the role of the state, but to seek to combine state power with class power from below, in a system of 'dual power' which brings into play an array of popular forces, parties, trade unions, workers' councils, local government, women's groups, black caucuses, activists of every sort, in a democratic exercise of power and maximum self-government in the productive process and every sphere of life. But the state must have an important role in the whole process... not only to contain and subdue reactionary resistance to socialist advance, but to fulfil many different functions, including arbitration between the diverse and possibly conflictual forces subsumed under the rubric "popular power"... It is upon the state and its diverse local and regional organs that will fall the task of providing the *ultimate* protection of political, civic and social rights; and it is the state that will be the *ultimate* recourse against manifestations of sexism, racism, discrimination, and abuses of power which will hardly be unknown even after capitalism has been transcended.'

The question of people's power in the state, their struggle for 'political supremacy' or state power, is absolutely central to any struggle for a better life for the common people. There is no way a serious people's movement can avoid the question of political power. The real issue here is the concrete forms of struggle for it. This, obviously, cannot be settled beforehand; the objectives and the forms of struggle to be adopted or combined depends on the specific and ever changing historical circumstances. While the revolutionary tradition has a great deal to offer here, the formula remains that of the great tactician Napoleon Bonaparte which Lenin was fond of reiterating: '*On s'engage et puis on voil*' (we join the battle and then we'll see)'. But there is one issue here which, though noted earlier, deserves a more specific reference, namely, the pursuit of revolutionary politics in regimes of more or less developed bourgeois democracy, where participation in parliamentary politics has posed so many intractable, still unresolved problems for the revolutionaries.

Problems here are far too many to be listed. The critics have pointed their accusing finger at the socialist and communist parties which, opting for parliamentary politics have steadily slid into reformism. Such participation breeds 'parliamentary cretinism', a naive equation of electoral victory with winning of power, even with radical change itself, so that there is no need for or interest any longer in developing a militant revolutionary movement. Whatever movements exist or are built outside are subordinated to the 'struggle' inside the parliament. The electoral success is bought at the cost of an ideological backslide which has lasting deleterious effect. Operating on the terrain of bourgeois politics, responding to issues it presents and accepting the choices it offers, entails a corruption of political consciousness and loss of revolutionary commitment. Criticism of bourgeois parties for failing by their own standards – a staple of parliamentary politics – almost invariably leads to endorsing these standards yourself so that your original concerns come to be given a go-by. The process of making yourself electable on the terms set by the establishment leads to mirroring establishment's view of the revolutionary left who are now seen as an embarrassment, when not treated with plain hostility. Parliamentary politics even as it corrupts in so many ways, exercises a most 'civilising' influence on revolutionaries, as Laski was fond of pointing out. It is no coincidence that the ruling classes looking for 'the most outstanding parliamentarians', or models of 'parliamentary rectitude', for their awards and honours have not unoften found them among leaders of socialist or communist parties. They are hailed by the mainstream media as 'statesmen' for their role as the best custodians of bourgeois politics. And so on.

That the ruling classes have been eminently successful in using democracy, its rights and institutions against the people and for promoting their own class interests and that the greatest enemy of democratisation in the world today, the U.S., can hawk 'democracy' around the world in support of its imperialist politics makes parliamentary politics all the more suspect in the eyes of its critics.

The critics are fully justified in what they say, but their criticism does not add up to a justification for any kind of 'anti-parliamentary cretinism', the in-principle rejection of parliamentary politics by certain ultra-left sections of the revolutionary movement. What we have here are problems that have to be confronted and resolved in terms of revolutionary vigilance in theory and practice and not evaded in a cretinous rejection of 'bourgeois democracy'. Parliamentary politics and electoral struggles are not to be rejected, or even treated as mere defensive tactics for the working people. They are today an integral part of any long revolution. They do not necessarily prevent a revolutionary movement or party from establishing and functioning on its own terrain, the terrain of independent class-based people's politics, which even as it confronts bourgeois politics on the latter's terrain, in parliament or outside, uses it to pose its own issues and choices, in its own way, before the people – not just for some electoral gains but real political advance. In other words, there is nothing in bourgeois democracy or parliamentary politics that in itself prevents its being subordinated to the extra-parliamentary politics of a revolutionary party or movement. Parties or movements are indeed coming up today, notably in Latin-America, which are thus combining parliamentary and extra-parliamentary methods in pursuit of their revolutionary objectives.

The issue here is not commitment to democracy which has always been a vital part of the socialist agenda – and it is people who have fought for and won whatever democracy we have; and they need and value it most. Nor is it 'bourgeois democracy' – apropos which Miliband, with the bitter Soviet experience in mind, has written: 'Regimes which do, either by necessity or choice, depend on the suppression of all opposition and the stifling of all civic freedoms must be taken to represent a disastrous regression, in political terms, from bourgeois democracy, whatever the economic and social achievements of which they must be capable... The civic freedoms which, however inadequately, form part of bourgeois democracy are the product of centuries of unremitting popular struggles. The task of Marxist politics is to defend these freedoms and to make possible their enlargement by the removal of their class boundaries.' It is not even that parliamentary politics, as a form of politics, has its possibilities in the struggle for socialism and cannot be rejected so long as these possibilities remain unexhausted, not in your theory but in people's own practical experience, and, therefore, as a general principle, participation in parliamentary politics is necessary whenever and wherever possible – though exceptions to this principle are admissible in specific historical situations when people's interests, interests of their revolutionary movement so demand. The real issue here is an approach distant both from ultra-leftism on the one hand and from social democratic politics of accommodation on the other. It is the principle, but without any exception this time, that parliamentary politics needs always to be subordinated to extra-parliamentary class and mass politics. It can never be over-emphasised that people's power grows only out of such politics, out of their own activity, organisation and struggles as these come to be suffused with revolutionary socialist consciousness.

It may be added that participation in parliamentary politics does not by itself or necessarily mean accepting the prevalent social order. Engels had categorically stated: 'the political freedoms, the right of assembly and association and the freedom of the press – these are our weapons. Are we to sit back and abstain when somebody tries to rob us of them? It is said that a political act on our part implies that we accept the existing state of affairs. On the contrary, so long as this state of affairs offers us the means of protesting against it, our use of these means does not signify that we recognise the prevailing order.' These means, including participation in parliamentary politics can in fact be used to redefine and extend the democratic parameters of the prevailing order in favour of the revolutionary movement, its extra-parliamentary struggles.

A Marxist perspective on the revolutionary process does not pose the issue of struggle for socialism, as its simplistic or ignorant critics think, in terms of violence or non-violence or insurrectionist versus non-insurrectionist strategy. For it the real issue is an articulation and relationship between two terrains of struggle, that waged *within* the existing institutions of bourgeois democracy, and that waged *outside* them, in which the latter is always and ultimately the *decisive* terrain. Such was the perspective of Lenin, the principle underlying his notion of 'dual power'. Conceptualised by him in relation to the revolutionary process in Russia, 'dual power' has generally been taken to mean an adversary relation between a revolutionary movement operating in a revolutionary situation, and a bourgeois government under challenge from that movement. But it is suggestive of a more basic principle in relation to the two terrains of struggle mentioned above, in which the latter is always and ultimately the decisive terrain. This Leninist position still holds. (Such also was the perspective of Gramsci, though he has not been spared a reformist reading to locate the decisive terrain of struggle within existing institutions).

Arguing that 'the centrepiece of the Leninist strategy is the principle of *dual power* which may or may not culminate in an explosive urban insurrectionism as the final act tipping the scales, as it were', Achin Vanaik has thus elucidated the Leninist perspective: 'The Leninist perspective argues not for counterposing the two terrains of struggle and choosing one or the other, but insists that at some point in the struggle within existing institutions (well below the "critical point") the key centres of power and their power wielders will polarise to the right, and the strategy of capture or transformation of the bourgeois state from within can go no further. The decisive terrain of struggle lies outside, between the "core" sectors – the top echelons of civil bureaucracy, of the courts, of the executive and the military – of the bourgeois state and the embryonic and emerging organs of an alternative state i.e. the emergence of a dual power situation which has to be resolved one way or the other...'

And here, while struggle within existing institutions remains a very important complement to the overall struggle, historical experience is, in its own way, quite instructive and needs to be taken note of. The presence of Soviets as effective organs of *dual power*, a power outside of existing institutions, was an important factor in the success of the October Revolution. Similar organs of potential or actual dual power emerged later in several other revolutionary processes too – in the Finnish Revolution and Bela Kun's Hungary in 1918, in 1919-23 Germany, in Italy in 1920, in Spain in 1936, in Chile in 1972-73, in Portugal in 1974-75 and so on. Their lack of effective power was a contributory factor in the ultimate dismal outcomes. Details apart, what historical experience the world over points to is the paramount need to build up people's organised strength, a social power, on the terrain outside the established institutions of bourgeois democracy as necessary sanctions for the success of the revolutionary process. This will also be an important factor in determining how peaceful or 'non-violent' this revolutionary process is going to be.

The issue under discussion has been well posed by Norman Geras. He has distinguished between the two main strategic perspectives for revolution in bourgeois democratic regimes which he calls the 'gateway' and 'bastion' hypotheses. Both hypotheses comprehend, as necessary for any minimally serious strategic approach, both a parliamentary and an extra-parliamentary dimension, both a continuity and discontinuity of political forms. But they still differ, and critically in this: the former (gateway) hypothesis forbids what the latter one countenances, 'a point of constitutional rupture'. In other words, the first hypothesis argues that the road to social revolution runs through the institutions of bourgeois democracy. The second argues that this is possible only up to a point beyond which the road will be blocked and the bourgeois democratic state reveal its essential character as a 'bastion' or 'fortress' against social revolution, which bastion then needs to be destroyed or overcome. The first perspective entertains no such possibility or need and the obvious implication is that extra-parliamentary struggles though allowed, must be geared and subordinated to parliamentary politics, to politics within the institutions of bourgeois democracy. The second perspective, acknowledging the possibility of a violent, extra-democratic showdown or resistance in the end game situation even in advanced bourgeois democracies, postulates the need to prepare for it so that such showdown or resistance by the dominant classes is effectively confronted and overcome. The second is obviously the right perspective for pursuit of revolutionary politics in regimes of bourgeois democracy.

As we have noted earlier, Marx himself had warned that even in countries with the possibility of a relatively peaceful socialist revolution, the ruling classes will not give in without staging 'a slave-holders revolt'. Engels had written: 'the time for surprise attacks, of revolutions carried out by small conscious minorities at the head of unconscious masses is past. When it is a question of complete transformation of the social organisation, the masses themselves must also be in it, must themselves already have grasped what is at stake, what they are going in for with body and soul.' He had urged the socialists to 'first win the great mass of the people'. Even so, he did not rule out a violent capitalist reaction to any peaceful bid for power – 'a blood-letting like that of 1871 in Paris'. The obvious implication is that extra-parliamentary struggles, the essential basis of any serious preparation to meet such a contingency, cannot and must not be subordinated to parliamentary politics. Mass extra-parliamentary socio-political movements and struggles indeed remain the central axis, the decisive terrain of the struggle for a socialist revolution. In fact capitalism is itself, by definition, and very effectively in its mode of acting and functioning, an extra-parliamentary force, and the capitalist state holds within itself any number of forces not amenable to the conventional democratic or parliamentary control. 'The "dominant class" is not a figure of speech', Miliband has pointed out, 'it denotes a very real and formidable concentration of power, a close partnership of capital and the capitalist state, a combined force of class power and state power, armed with vast resources, and determined to use them to the full, in conjunction with its allies abroad, to prevent an effective challenge to its power.' There will be no advance whatsoever until the working people's movement is activated in the form of becoming capable of *offensive* action – as against the usual defensive action through conventional trade unionism, party politics in parliament or outside, etc. – against capital and the dominant classes through its own appropriate institutions and through its extra-parliamentary force, its organised and conscious social power in society.

Here indeed also lies the answer to the question how violent or peaceful, armed insurrectionary or otherwise, the revolutionary process will be. Violence is not the essence of the matter and there is nothing unMarxist or irrational in seeking to carry through a revolutionary process without violence or force of arms. But its possibility depends, above all, upon whether the ruling classes will allow it to be non-violent or peaceful. Historical experience, October Revolution included, bears witness that they will not. (Chile is a classic example in more recent times). Even so, the greater the strength of the extra-parliamentary force or social power the revolutionaries have, the more evident their ability and willingness to meet counter revolutionary violence with overwhelming revolutionary violence, the greater the chance that violence can be avoided and the revolutionary process be relatively peaceful.

The amount of violence that will be involved in a given revolutionary process is indeed impossible to predict in advance. It depends on the one hand on the nature and amount of ruling class resistance but in a large part, also, on how successfully the socialists have built people's social power from below and how hegemonic or influential they are in society as a whole. As Wilhelm Reich has argued, 'the larger the mass base of the revolutionary movement, the less violence will be required and the more, also, will the masses lose their fear of revolution. The increasing degree of influence of the revolutionary movement inside the army and the state apparatus has the same effect. For this reason the Russian revolution had only a minimum of casualties.' (Bourgeois propaganda's violence in the Russian revolution did not accompany but *followed* the revolution, thanks to the foreign-backed armed counter-revolution by the former ruling classes).

For socialists or communists, revolution is a matter, not of violence or non-violence, but of fundamental structural change in society. As revolutionaries they do not *advocate* violence. For them it is a tragic necessity to defend revolution with violence when the ruling classes violate the victories and rights of the people. People have a natural aversion to violence and revolutionaries respect it – a respect, as Trotsky has underlined in his account of the Russian Revolution, the Bolsheviks remarkably demonstrated in 1917.

The two issues discussed above directly or indirectly involve the key question of struggle for power in the state. This brings into focus the issue of party, of revolutionary leadership in the struggle for socialism.

The collapse of the Soviet Union and the ignominious disintegration of the Soviet Communist Party naturally caused a crisis in the world communist movement, with one party after another disintegrating or degenerating into social democracy, and a question mark hanging over the future of the few which have, much disoriented, survived, often in name only. These parties born of the Third International and strongly influenced by the particularities of the Bolshevik Party, emphasised unity, discipline and centralisation and had significant achievements including revolutions to their credit. But their ties to the Soviet Union limiting their initiative and theoretical development, they were already in decline, increasingly incapable of playing the revolutionary role they claimed for themselves. Now they or their successors are seen to have become irrelevant for any radical purposes. Much the same is true of Social Democratic parties. They too have failed to deliver on their promises. Degenerating steadily on the road to reformism since the collapse of Second International at the time of the First World War, they have now fully accommodated themselves to the neo-liberal agenda of global capitalism – epitomised now by 'New' Labour in Britain. Organisationally, these parties are seen as top-down bureaucratic structures, illustrating as it were

Michels' 'law of oligarchy', inevitably autonomous of the working people they claim to represent and marked by a gulf between leadership and ordinary members, between 'officers' and 'the rank and file' as Michels described them. One consequence of it all is a questioning on the Left of the very *raison d'etre* of the party, its appropriateness as a political platform for radical action. Voices have been heard to say that parties have had their day, that they were inherently undemocratic and therefore poor instruments for any democratic social transformation, that they were much too integrated into a parliamentary system which itself has outlived its historical relevance, and so on. Instead, it is argued that the struggles of the Left would best be waged by more democratically or consensually constituted social movements, concerned with gender, race, the environment, peace, culture and such other issues. What the Left needs is not party or parties but a 'greening' of its politics that these concerns demand. This however is a bit too simplistic, lacking awareness of the real needs of the Left.

The social movements are of course a very welcome development. Their emergence has been in Miliband's somewhat sharp expression, 'a dramatic vote of no confidence in the ability of labour movements and socialist parties to represent adequately or at all, the grievances, interests and demands of... the constituencies which they have mobilised'. Their criticism of the Left parties is generally valid and has forced upon them questions they had in an earlier epoch tended to relegate to the periphery of their concerns or to ignore altogether. By themselves they have been active as agencies of pressure and protest, occasionally even of radical struggle. It is also a fact that many on the Left in recent years have found involvement in social movements to be both far more politically effective and more personally satisfying than life in the existing political parties. These movements thus continue to be needed and even in their present form will continue to remain a valuable component of forces on the Left. But they are no alternative to party or parties of the Left which remain of primary importance as a potential, if not actual, instrument of socialist advance.

Their questionable internal democracy apart, focussed as they are on a single issue or sector of social problems, the social movements are much too fragmented and partial in their perspectives and struggles to cohere together to provide leadership to any society-wide struggle, to be a needed substitute for a socialist/communist party or parties. It has been pointed out that even when they have come together, along with other non-party movements or organisations like the progressive trade unions – in forms that range from the Rainbow Coalition in the USA and the Action Canada Network in Canada to the Anti-WTO Movement or Platform of People's Movements in India and the Opposition to the Devastation Caused by the World Bank/IMF in Sri Lanka or such things as World Social Forum – it has been mainly of 'popular front'-style strategic networking between the top leaderships of the various organisations. What has been missing – and this is now strongly felt by many social movement leaders themselves – is something that is more than the sum of the parts, something which a party alone can provide and which Communist and Social Democratic parties did partly provide in their hey day. The kind of socialist organisations that are required at any point of time is always linked with the kind of tasks required to be carried out. And that is how in the constellation of forces and organisations on the Left, party or parties retain their *decisive* importance. They are needed to affirm a socialist presence, to advance socialist alternatives, to inscribe immediate demands and grievances into a larger framework, to mount a moral and intellectual challenge to capitalist hegemony, and to provide leadership to a society-wide struggle for socialism.

The whole history of worldwide revolutionary movement shows that the struggle cannot be waged and political power won and maintained without the organisation and leadership that a revolutionary party provides – the example is there in all the successful revolutions of our time. This history is also replete with examples of failure of alternatives to the revolutionary party as a means of achieving the overthrow of capitalism, be it social democracy in the German revolution in 1918, voluntarism of Che Guevara's guerrilla foco in Bolivia in 1967, spontaneism of the student-led urban revolt in France in the late sixties (with its rejection of organisation, authority and above all of the political party), or 'popular front' strategy (and peaceful transition to socialism) put to test in the shape of the Popular Unity government of Salvador Allende in Chile in early seventies. Among the several subjective and objective determinants of these failures, the lack of a well organised mass revolutionary party was certainly one of the most important. (A different kind of example is the historical experience of the United States, a country without a mass-based socialist party where, even though there is no shortage of social or grass roots movements, conservatism holds sway and has been hugely successful in warding off any serious challenge from the Left).

The need for a revolutionary party of socialism can never be overemphasised. Well described as 'the concrete expression of the Marxist synthesis of determinism and voluntarism in revolutionary practice', it has to be a party which is capable of bringing together under socialist hegemony all the actual and potential anti-capitalist forces in society, including the new social movements, and mobilising and leading the mass of the working people in their struggle for political supremacy in the state; it has to be party which aims to achieve representation within existing institutions but which is even more actively involved in actions and struggles outside and can successfully articulate *all* the different forms of struggle in pursuit of its revolutionary objectives; it has to be a party whose revolutionary politics accommodates other parties of the left, other emancipatory visions, movements, militant groups and organisations, in a consensus which is democratic within and without, where parties establish their revolutionary legitimacy or vanguard role not by self-proclamation but by their political practice and public sanction, and those preferring to practise democratic centralism, practise it on the basis of the widest inner-party democracy and do not let it degenerate into non-revolutionary authoritarianism. It may be that the notion of a single, vanguard, all-encompassing party of the Left has had its day. But the vanguard role and organisation in the revolutionary process retain their crucial importance even if the precise forms of realisation of either are variable and do not preclude a plurality of revolutionary socialist or communist political parties and organisations, indeed any kind of organisation, say a 'front' that does the same work. As one suggestion has it, it can be a coalition but one 'with a core, a solid centre, ... to be provided by the representatives of a socialist party able to exercise a major influence on the coalition, without any presumption of a privileged position'. This is crucially important because the struggle for power involves, daily and ultimately, a confrontation with the bourgeois state which, in *all* its forms, is itself *the vanguard organisation* of the dominant classes. The revolutionary vanguard organisation, however constituted, is the precise counterpoint to the bourgeois state, the most effective weapon with which to confront and defeat it. This is a role which cannot be performed by social democratic parties, or by small groups, even if they call themselves parties, self-confined in their sectarian ghettoes, or by the surviving communist parties unless they are radically transformed. The building up of party or parties able to play this role, parties capable of providing the necessary revolutionary leadership to the struggle for socialism has to be a key task on the agenda of the left today in different countries.

The classical Marxist tradition, with its focus on the centrality, progressively so, of the working class to the strategic alignment of forces in the struggle for socialism, viewed the revolutionary party as essentially a party of the working class, which with Lenin also came to be defined as the proletarian vanguard. There is a complexity of more than one category here and in view of the changing structure, and the role, inclinations, and capacities of the working class in late capitalism, the Leninist concept of the revolutionary party as the vanguard working class party needs to be carefully reassessed. But it certainly cannot be casually questioned or discarded as many on the Left have urged us to do. But if the concept, however reassessed especially in relation to vanguardism, still remains relevant for countries of advanced capitalism, with their majority or strategically significant presence of the working class, strictly viewed, this cannot be said to be the case in countries of peripheral or semi-peripheral capitalism. Their historical experience also indicates otherwise. The revolutionary parties in the third world, and some of them even made successful revolutions under the banner of Marxism, have had no primary focus on the numerically small working class nor its preponderance among members, cadre or leadership. Along with intellectuals they came not from the working class but mostly from other oppressed sections of society. They can be said to be working class parties only in the sense that they were guided by Marxism, which in a most important sense is a working class theory or ideology or world view – the important thing therefore being not a literally 'working class party' but a revolutionary party led by Marxism. This is not a subject I need to pursue any further. The point of my argument is to emphasise, rather re-emphasise the need for a Marxism-led mass revolutionary party based on and representing the interests of all exploited people including the working class – the victims of global capitalism in its specific manifestations in different countries – and capable of organising and mobilising them for power in the state and a socialist transformation of society. I would however like to return to Marx and Lenin, most briefly, to underline a few additional considerations in this regard.

Though involved in educating and organising the working class, party as such never became a major concern for Marx. There is vagueness and variety in his use of the term 'party' – a scholar, Monty Johnston, has identified as least five possible models. It is, therefore, not possible to construct any single or systematic theory of the party in Marx. But he was most emphatic about two things: the need for a party of the working class and the independenceof a working class party. Marx repeatedly suggested that the workers cannot be regarded as a class in the full sense of the term until they have created teir own distinct party. Quite early, in *Communist Manifesto*, he wrote of 'the organisation of the proletarians into a class, and consequently into a political party...', just as he saw the 'immediate aim' of all proletarian parties to be the 'formation of the proletarians into a class'. In their Address to the Central Authority of the (Communist) League, Marx and Engels wrote:

"The German workers are not able to attain power and achieve their own class interests without completely going through a lengthy revolutionary development... they themselves must do the utmost for the final victory by making it clear to themselves what their class interests are, by taking up their position as an independent party and by not allowing themselves to be misled for a single moment... into refraining from the independent organisation of the party of the proletariat.' A couple of decades later, in 1871, basing himself on the historical experience of the working class movement in the intervening period, Marx wrote: 'In its struggle against the collective power of the propertied classes, the working class cannot act, as a class, except by constituting itself into a political party, distinct from and opposed to all old parties formed by the propertied classes'. He regarded 'this constitution of the proletariat into a political party (as) indispensable in order to ensure the triumph of the social revolution'. And it is historical experience again which led Marx to argue that 'the workers' party must act in the most organised, most unanimous and most independent fashion possible if it is not to be exploited and taken in tow by the bourgeoisie.' (In much the same manner, holding that to preach abstention from politics to workers is 'to throw them into the embrace of bourgeois politics', Engels had always insisted that 'the workers' party must never be the Fagtail of any bourgeois party; it must be independent and have its own goal, and its own policy'.)

Yet, possibly due to a certain economic determinism which along with optimism of a revolutionary underlay his estimate of the revolutionary potential of the working class, Marx failed to realise the full importance of the party. He had a somewhat simplified, over-optimistic view of the transformation of the working class from a 'class-in-itself' into a 'class-for-itself', that is a class theoretically aware of its objective situation, class interests and historical role. Crucial here was the assumption, Marx's concern for 'educating' the workers notwithstanding, that political, i.e. socialist consciousness arises almost spontaneously from the economic circumstances and struggle of the workers, accompanied by an underestimation of the expanding role of bourgeois ideology and the dangers of growing political reformism among the working classes, and therefore, an underestimation of the need to combat both. It is these and related weaknesses that were later overcome, above all, by Lenin's theory of the Party which even as an advance was a break both with Marx's concept of organisation in which the distinction between party and class remained blurred and with the orthodox social democratic conception of the party as representing the class.

Lenin recognised the importance of organisation and theorised it as no Marxist revolutionary had done before him. 'In its struggle for power', wrote Lenin, 'the proletariat has no other weapon but its organisation.' His activist attitude to revolution-making also led him to focus on the crucial question of 'socialist consciousness', its acquisition by the proletariat so that it indeed becomes a 'class-for-itself'. 'Revolutions are *prepared*', Lenin was to later shout at the Italian delegation during the Second Congress of the Comintern, telling them: you cannot reap what you have not sown. For Lenin, building a well-organised and ideologically well-equipped party was central to this preparation, irrespective of how the future revolution is conceived.

Lenin elaborated his theory of the Party in *What Is To Be Done*? There were later refinements as also 'serious ambiguities and contradictions' of his final years, negative intrusions from a most difficult historical period and not, as critics have argued, inherent in his original conception. Distinguished from particular aspects reflecting the specificities of the Russian situation, the essentials of Lenin's organisational theory are all there, and as Le Blanc has suggested, the general argument of *What Is To Be Done*?, despite its polemical exaggerations, remains reasonable and valuable for later periods, including our own: the absolutely independent organisation of the advanced workers, a revolutionary vanguard, functioning on the basis of democratic centralism, committed to raising the general level of working class consciousness, upholding the overall interests of workers and all exploited, and organising proletariat-led class struggle for the purpose of winning political power and of replacing capitalism by a socialist organisation of society. The perspective underlying Lenin's theory is of a mass and class movement led by a vanguard party, having the closest possible relationship with the mass of workers via leadership in struggle. The emphasis is on activity of the masses and the party leads from within and not standing outside them. The party is a vanguard in the sense that in a period of struggle, there has to be a 'most advanced resolute section' which 'pushes forward all others', which 'theoretically (should) have over the great mass of the proletariat the advantage of clearly understanding the line of march, the conditions, and the ultimate general results of the proletarian movement'. And 'democratic centralism' Lenin defined as 'unity of action, freedom of discussion and criticism'. The Bolsheviks under Lenin had institutionalised tendency or faction rights within their party.

The organisational vision underlying Lenin's conception of a vanguard party is that of a determined and principled but also an open and evolving group of revolutionaries, with a variety of critical minded individuals who are committed to working together for a common goal, through a collectively (democratically) directed effort. Insofar as there can be no prospect of revolution – no matter how this revolution is conceived – in the absence of a revolutionary party, this vision remains relevant and if certain specific aspects of Lenin's theory of the Party rightly need to be reassessed in the light of historical experience, the principles behind them remain valid. There are no guarantees in Lenin that the party indeed represents what it claims to represent or that its formulation of interests of revolution or the guidance it provides to the movement is necessarily correct. Nor is it that party is in possession of a ready-made truth which it injects unilaterally into the class or mass movement and which establishes beyond question its right to leadership. All this requires to be verified in practice. In fact central to Lenin's conception is party's close relationship with the masses of working people, mutual interaction between the two in which the party learns from the class and the masses by direct participation in their struggles, even as it performs its role as leaders and educators. The party leads, as already mentioned, from within and not by standing outside the struggling masses. The reciprocity in the relation between the party and the working people is a necessary principle of party's theoretical and practical activity, including all agitational work. Warning against agitation becoming 'a noisy monologue', Trotsky wrote: 'Agitation is not only the means of communicating to the masses this or that slogan calling the masses to action, and so on. For a party, agitation is also a means of lending an ear to the masses, of sounding out its moods and thoughts... For the Marxists, the Leninists, *agitation is always a dialogue with the masses*'. The vanguard role of the party itself depends on its preparedness to learn from the masses by responding positively to the plurality of opinions, the internal moods of the masses. Only thus can it compensate and correct mistakes, rectify omissions in programme and struggles, ensure flexibility and speed of response in diverse and rapidly changing situations.

Three issues or principles in Lenin's theory of party need to be specifically noted and underlined. There is the notion of 'vanguard' organisation or role which remains relevant as a principle, indeed indispensable so long as the bourgeois state exists and there is the need for coordination of popular struggles and responses, for political centralisation, to confront it. Its precise expression, as a matter of historical development of the revolutionary movement, is variable. As mentioned above, it is not necessarily representable only by a single revolutionary socialist or communist party. Vanguard organisation or role could as well be expressed through many such parties or organisations coming together in an effective united front or through different tendencies within a single vanguard party or through some other appropriate combination. In fact the precise forms of expression are not so important as that vanguard status or role has to be politically vindicated and deserved in the eyes of the people, not imposed from above but earned by active struggles on behalf of people, by actual performance, if need be in competition with other parties. A revolutionary organisation claims leadership or vanguard role not as a right or by self-definition (or by law or constitutional enfranchisement), it fights to win it, in practice, in struggle, by its clearsightedness, integrity and behaviour, its entire political and moral image as the best fighter for or defender of the people. Equally relevant remains the principle of 'democratic centralism'. The principle has been much abused in the communist movement and no useful generalisations can be made as to the specific organisational structure to ensure it, except to insist on its flexibility. But there is no alternative to its combination of 'freedom of discussion' and 'unity of action' in facing a highly centralised enemy on diverse fronts, namely the state power of the ruling classes. And then there is the overarching principle, the very *raison d'etre* of a revolutionary party, its independence, which Lenin, with Marx, never ceased to emphasise, and without which no kind of revolutionary or vanguard role is possible – 'under all circumstances uphold the independence of the proletarian movement even if it is in its most embryonic form', Lenin had insisted at the Second Congress of the Communist International. The independence of the revolutionary party is never to be sacrificed to any other political force, bourgeois, centrist or reformist. Such independence however does not preclude alliances, compromises, temporary arrangements in pursuit of revolutionary politics but it most definitely precludes giving up the right to free criticism, a separate political line and of course a separate organisation. These essential principles of Lenin's organisational theory do not necessarily make for an elitist, hierarchical or bureaucratic party, inherently authoritarian, and inimical to 'creativity in diversity', as critics have continued to argue. Instead, they focus on the central function of a revolutionary party which is to act as a politically coordinating and centralising force, which brings together the separate, fragmentary or partial struggles of the working classes as well as struggles or movements of other oppressed classes and sections of the people, in a revolutionary opposition in order to regularly and ultimately confront 'the collective power of the propertied classes', the 'politically centralising instance' of bourgeois society, the bourgeois state. This in fact is the fundamental concern of Lenin's theory of the Party, for he saw the revolutionary movement as based on an alliance of all oppressed sections of society, a 'revolutionary alliance of the oppressed', he had called it. For Lenin the party member's 'ideal should not be a trade-union secretary, but a *tribune of the people*, able to react to every manifestation of tyranny and oppression, no matter where it takes place, no matter what stratum or class of the people it affects; he must be able to group all these manifestations into a single picture of police violence and capitalist exploitation; he must be able to take advantage of every petty event in order to explain his socialistic convictions and his (socialist) demands to *all*, in order to explain to *all* and everyone the world-historic significance of the struggle for the emancipation of the proletariat.' He who forgets, said Lenin, that 'the Communists support every revolutionary movement' and are for that reason obliged 'to expound and emphasise *general democratic tasks before the whole people*, without for a moment concealing our socialistic convictions' is not a Communist. And for that matter, not a socialist today.

Lenin's theory of the Party is part of a much larger complex of thought and action called Leninism. A recognition of the relevance of this theory today, if it includes rejection of dogmatic Stalinist interpretations, also excludes any uncritical adulation of Lenin or endorsement of his ideas. Whatever he said or did here, or for that matter elsewhere, his entire legacy – 'a passionate and complex cultural tradition of revolutionary theory and practice', in the words of Shiela Rowbotham – needs to be addressed *critically*, in the best classical sense of that term; that is, it has to be reassessed, reworked, reappropriated or renewed, in the light of historical experience and in relation to our tasks of the day. This, naturally, also requires its integration with the insights developed by other revolutionary leaders, pre-eminently by Mao Tse-tung and including Gramsci and such revolutionary critics as Rosa Luxemburg. Even so Leninism proper remains a legacy we particularly need to hold on to today. For, as Lukacs in his excellent summary of Leninism has argued, 'the core of Lenin's thought and his decisive link with Marx' is the belief in 'the actuality of the revolution', the belief that revolution is a real historical possibility and that political action – the conscious voluntary struggle for socialism by revolutionaries – makes a huge and decisive difference.

A Few Final Comments

Crisis of socialism today is really a crisis of the social revolution of our times – a revolution which remains necessary if humanity is to survive and make further progress. Even in the failure of its first efforts, it has left the world significantly changed for the better, and though in crisis, it has enough resources left for a resumed struggle for socialism. The proper socialist response to the crisis is neither to mourn the passing of 'actually existing socialism', nor to seek answers in the so-called 'socialism of the market' which can only produce new versions of capitalism. Lessons of course have to be learnt from what went wrong in the past. The proper response however is to set about building the socialist movement of the future.

The reasons which in the first place gave rise to the movement for socialism still hold, more so at the beginning of this century than they did at the beginning of the last or at any time earlier. Capitalism remains a deeply exploitative and ecologically disastrous way of organising social life. Apparently triumphant, capitalism continues to operate under the same structural compulsions, producing the same catastrophic consequences as before. It remains ridden with crises and congenitally unable to subordinate its achievements to the needs of human beings, unable, despite its prodigious productive abilities, to offer even bare survival to vast majorities in the world it dominates. Despite its current apotheosis, capitalism has resolved none of the problems which have for more than a century and a half given sustenance to socialist aspirations and struggles. The logic favouring a worldwide transition to socialism remains as compelling today as it has ever been.

The collapse in the Soviet Union does not in any way change this logic, except that the economically exploitative, morally repulsive and ecologically unsustainable character of capitalism is now more apparent than at any time in its history. The Cuban writer Pablo Armando, when asked about how the collapse in the East was being interpreted by the United States, wrote: 'They are happy now. They are celebrating. For them the world has ended. History has ended. How very silly to think that! Communism has not disappeared. The utopias of socialism and communism are not going to disappear as long as there are exploiters and exploited. You have to be very happy having one piece of bread to eat while others throw meat to their dogs. I didn't have to read Marx to know the difference.' Even as the enemies were, once again, declaring socialism dead, Eduardo Galeano had warned against claiming too much for what had happened. In their rush to the funeral, they are burying the wrong corpse, he had commented. Socialism was not born with the Soviet Union, but a long time before it, with capitalism – as a response to, indeed the negation of capitalism. Socialism cannot be dead as long as capitalism lives. Given its ineradictable contradictions and limitations, capitalism guarantees that men and women everywhere will continue to search for alternatives to it; and socialism continues to represent the only rational and humane alternative to capitalism. Our business as socialists, now more than ever, is to defend and advance that alternative, to resume the 'journey of hope', a 'shared search' for human emancipation as Raymond Williams called it.

II

The objective conditions and more than an embryonic subjectivity at individual and mass organisational levels exist for the reconstruction of a socialist opposition to the currently dominant capitalist system. In the West the euphoria over 'no alternative' is long over. The declaration of 'the end of history', like similar declarations in the past, stands rejected as so much silliness. The long moment people thought typical, the welfarist capitalism is recognised as not typical, typical is the harsh reality they are now experiencing. People are learning the hard way what capitalism is really about. Just as in the hinterlands of global capitalism, ravaged by 'globalisation' and subjected to the new domination of America, people are learning anew about capitalsim and imperialism, and about the compradorism of their own ruling elites. The question of an alternative is back on the agenda, and in different shapes and forms, in however confused or muddled a manner, anti-capitalist struggles are being resumed in different parts of the world. These struggles may not produce a remake of the previous century. History does not repeat itself, we are told. But 'history is more imaginative than we are', Marx had said. History certainly has its surprises – and revolutions by the oppressed and exploited are among them.

Revolution is not only armed struggle or insurrection, though it still cannot be ruled out. It does not at all help to see revolution as a punctual moment in history or in terms of iconic images like the taking of the Winter Palace or storming of the Bastille. Revolution is best understood as a complex process of social transformation–with special complexities of its own in regimes of bourgeois democracy. And however we understand it, we cannot predict the practical and theoretical forms of the revolutions of the future. But we know the surprises that vicissitudes of world history brought us in the twentieth century. And there is no reason to doubt that this one will bring more. The inventiveness of masses in revolt has been and will continue to be beyond the imagination of the most sensitive scholar or philosopher.

Revolution is not over. The basic conflicts between classes, between the oppressed and the oppressors, between a new and the old social order will not cease because the Soviet Union has ceased to be and a Fukuyama has announced the 'end of history'. The dynamics and forces which generated the revolutions of the twentieth century remain as they were in the past. The end of 'historical communism' has not put an end to poverty or to people's thirst for justice. The poor and forsaken of the third world still hope for a better life. Not exactly enthusiastic over revolutions, past or future, Fred Halliday, in his recent study on the subject, has yet pointed to 'the enduring inability of those with power and wealth to comprehend the depth of hostility to them' and 'the ability of history... to surprise', and written: 'the agenda of the revolutions of modern history is still very much with us because the aims they asserted... are far from having been achieved.' This leaves revolution still on the agenda of history. Revolution remains the vital truth, the unfinished story of our times – in whatever shape or form and over however long a period the rest of the story may be told.

This however has not prevented scholars of different persuasions and calibres from preaching that revolution is over. Along with men of 'science' of Marxism, in Russia and outside, they have even been asking if Russia would not have been better off without October Revolution, as if Lenin or Bolsheviks, or the Russian people, had any other choice. The question is in any case irrelevant and not worth discussing. But there is a point I would still like to make about these scholars' failure to understand October Revolution and, for that matter, any other revolution or revolutionary process.

Revolutions have their historical causation. But revolutions don't happen because of neat economic or political, personal or social calculations, or as a result of some one's 'scientific' theorising about it. Even Lenin's formula, 'revolutions occur when those below do not accept any longer to be ruled as before and those above cannot rule any longer as before' does not capture – and in my opinion was never meant to capture – the full reality of what happens, nor does 'this consideration' as Dr. Johnson once put it, 'that if the abuse be enormous, nature will rise up and claiming her original rights overturn a corrupted political system.' Revolutions happen because an oppressive system has become unbearable *and* there are people ready to bring it down – people with a dream of better life, 'Traum' Marx called it, who are willing and prepared to lay down their lives for it. Drawing attention specifically to the latter aspect, Teodor Shanin has observed: 'Social scientists often miss a centrepiece of any revolutionary struggle – the fervour and anger which drives revolutionaries and makes them into what they are.

Academic training and bourgeois convention deaden its appreciation. The "phenomenon" cannot be easily "operationalised" into factors, tables and figures... Yet, without this factor, any understanding of revolutions falls flat. That is why clerks, bankers, generals, and social scientists so often fail to see revolutionary upswing even when looking at it directly. At the very centre of revolution lies an emotional upheaval of moral indignation, revulsion, and fury with the powers-that-be, such that one cannot demur or remain silent, whatever the cost. Within its glow, for a while, men surpass themselves, breaking the shackles of intuitive self-preservation, convention, day-to-day convenience, and routine'. I would only add that the essential thrust of Shanin's observations holds irrespective of how revolution or revolutionary process is understood or visualised.

III

Capitalism has indeed shown remarkable resilience and survived beyond what can be described as its historical time. But its survival has now put a question mark over the future of humankind. Hobsbawm has written: 'If humanity is to have a recognisable future, it cannot be by prolonging the past or the present. If we try to build the third millennium on that basis, we shall fail. And the price of failure, that is to say, the alternative to a changed society, is darkness.' 'Darkness' yet does not capture the full gravity of what lies ahead. Caught in a global structural crisis, capitalism has become more creative than ever in unleashing its destructive potential. Its accumulative logic and America-led global politics are threatening humanity with unheard of ecological disasters and nuclear exterminism. With capitalism, humanity is indeed headed for a collective suicide and destruction of the earth itself. Socialism, therefore, is not just 'a changed society', a superior social order, it is today the necessary defence of humanity and our planet earth. This in its own way makes socialism all the more possible as an alternative to capitalism. Alternatives are discovered or invented, or even recovered when it becomes clear that we cannot survive without them. So it is now with socialism. Pointing to the human tragedy that capitalism's continued existence now portends for humankind, this is how Chomsky has put it in his characteristically simple manner: 'At this stage of history, either one of two things is possible. Either the general population will take control of its own destiny and will concern itself with community interests, guided by values of solidarity, sympathy, and concern for others, or, alternatively, there will be no destiny for anyone to control.'

Socialism is necessary and also an 'objective possibility' defined by the socio-economic conditions of capitalism and the alternative people may come to seek. But this does not imply its inevitability. Socialism is no inevitable product of any economic laws or something decreed by supposedly inexorable 'dialectics' – interpretations the critics have often foisted on Marx. There are no inevitabilities or guarantees of victory in Marxist theory of transition to socialism. It is the subjective factor, the conscious political intervention which is decisive in the actualisation of the possibility of socialism. Marxist socialists have never deemed inevitability or certainty of success indispensable for their struggle. As in the past so now, the possibility of socialism is spur enough for them to act and the perspective remains on the one hand of a long march guided and fired by the vision of a radically different society and on the other of a movement which learns and becomes more conscious as it advances and whose members do not mix up their own mortality with a timetable for the achievement of socialist goals; they know that history does not always deliver victories within your own lifetime. Daniel Singer has written:

> If we want to recover the dialectical link between the movement and its objective, we must draw clear distinctions between actuality, necessity, and inevitability. Socialism may be a historical *possibility*, or even *necessary* to eliminate the evils of capitalism, but this does not mean that it will *inevitably* take place. This departure from the fatalistic conception is, in a sense, a return to the more distant past, when socialism was not considered as bound to happen, since there was always the possibility, to quote the terms of Rosa Luxemburg, that barbarism would win out. Above all, uncertainty as to the ultimate result should not imply passivity, obedience, or resignation. On the contrary, it dictates greater

participation, more activity, and more militancy since, within limits of objective conditions, the future will be what we shall make it. And this renewed conviction and activism would be particularly welcome today, because the power of the ruling class and the arrogance of its ideologues is largely due to our weakness, to our surrender, to our acceptance of the established rules of the game.

IV

'Utopian' is the charge that continues to be made against socialism. In a sense, any political project is the affirmation of something that is not there, something, in short, imagined and therefore amenable to the charge of utopianism. But, obviously, this is not what the critics mean. Their real objective is to the nature of the socialist project, the transcendence of capitalism it seeks. There are those for whom any effort to move beyond the confines of capitalism is utopian – a position not too difficult to understand. As Arnold Thurman once put it: 'It may be asserted as a principle of human organisation that when new types of social organization are required, respectable, well-thought-of, and conservative people are unable to take part in them. Their moral and economic prejudices, their desire for the approval of other members of the group, compel them to oppose any form of organization which does not fit into the picture of society as they have known it in the past... Nothing seems clearer than that the attitudes of any given ruling class are so set that all arguments in the world will not change them.' But this obviously does not make the charge of 'utopianism' valid. There is however another argument which has a wider acceptance. It questions and rejects the socialist project of a viable, class-less and state-less, socialised property-based free and humane social order as an impossible ideal, something that does not and cannot exist, something never done or realised before; we simply cannot do without private property or classes, without a capitalist market or class-structure to make the economy work. This argument does carry weight with the ignorant and the unwary, the so-called 'average' citizens in thrall to the conventional bourgeois ways of thinking. But it is nevertheless a straw argument.

Our growing knowledge in the fields of ethnography and

anthropology, about human's present and past has much in it that shows this argument to be seriously flawed. Australian Aborigines have reportedly maintained for millennia a society in near perfect ecological balance, with no wars, ruling classes, or exploitation of each other and with minimal material wants satisfied with a minimum of work and a maximum of creatively used 'free time'. Evolutionist anthropology has generally supported the view that there were thousands of years of class-less, state-less non-patriarchal agricultural societies, some large and complex, before the origins of private property. We can indeed be said to have had the experience of socialism or 'primitive communism' several times longer than we have of class societies. This experience, in its absence of private property and classes, had a *humane* quality to it, something worth reappropriation, of course, in necessarily new forms – which suggests more than just viability of a socialist future for humankind. In one of his images of the society of the future this is indeed how Marx saw it. Marx thought of socialism/communism in terms of a 'process of human emancipation and recovery', 'as the complete return of man to himself as a *social* (i.e., human) being – a return become conscious, and accomplished within the entire wealth of previous development'.

This apart, it is a form of myopic conservative prejudice to think that everything which does not exist cannot exist. With the same 'logic' one could have stated that slavery was the only possible form of large-scale agricultural and handicraft production (in the 1st century A.D.); that monarchy was the only possible form of government (in the 14th and 15th century); that parliament could only be elected without universal franchise (in the 18th century) etc. Yet slavery finished by being abolished. Republics appeared while monarchies disappeared in their majority. Universal franchise ended by becoming general in all countries opting for a parliamentary system. Not to see what is developing without being already realised is a form of ideological colour-blindness often based upon wishful thinking; you don't see what you don't want to see.

Ernest Mandel has argued: 'The platitude that "Marxian

socialism" does not exist anywhere in the world today is tirelessly repeated, as in effect an argument against all human progress. But was it utopian to fight for the abolition of slavery, which existed on a large scale for more than a thousand years?... Religious oppression, including the burning of heretics at the stake, was a "fact of life" for at least five centuries. Was it then utopian to try to establish freedom of conscience and freedom of thought?... Why should it be utopian today to try to do away with wage labour and gigantic state bureaucracies, which after all have been central structures of society for no more than two hundred years?... Utopia, in the broad sense of the word, has been one of the great motors of the eventual achievement of historical progress.'

Any serious student of history would know that every significant social advance in history has at some point had to conquer the notion that it was impossible or that it had never been done before. Utopias are what have moved people throughout history to make it a better world. So it is now with socialism.

Theoretically, the possibility of socialism arises from within the contradictions of capitalism. Morally, opposition to capitalism is its own justification since capitalism is today poisoning human survival itself, let alone human happiness. The resolve to overturn this globally dominant system and build socialism does indeed involve 'utopian surplus' as Ernst Bloch once called it. The utopian dimension of the socialist project of course must not translate itself into either 'teleology' or 'messianic eschatology'. We must not be starry-eyed about the future and also need to divest ourselves of the hubris of tying our own mortality to its construction. But we must also not let the historically limited and capitalism-blighted vision of our enemies settle the question of possibilities of the future. 'Utopian' is a compliment and a challenge we should be willing to accept.

V

We, as socialists, are utopian but we are realistically utopian. Our project has its roots deep on the one hand in the reality of capitalism and on the other hand in people's economic, social and political struggles against it. Therefore even in our optimism about the possibility of socialism, we are not oblivious of possibilities of the other kind inherent in the present situation. The fact that our perspective is that of a long march does not mean that we have plenty of time to start moving. Crises are beginnings but they can be endings as well. It is quite possible that capitalism in crisis will begin to unravel at the seams at a time when we are still dishevelled and disorganised and thus incapable of steering the emerging struggles of the people into an affective overall struggle against capitalism. Popular discontent is rising, and if we, as socialists, do not provide rational and progressive solutions, there are plenty of people waiting in the wings with their irrational and reactionary solutions. The absence of an effective alternative to capitalist social order has already much-contributed to 'the flowering of poisonous weeds in the capitalist jungle' – racism, sexism, xenophobia, anti-semitism, ethnic hatreds, religious fundamentalisms, and things much worse. Fascism's rise to significance in western Europe in recent years is a warning that the ghosts of the past are not buried for ever, and similar ghosts are appearing elsewhere. The old choice, socialism or barbarism, may still lie in the future. But barbarism of sorts is already with us in the form of a globally degraded and plundered environment, of famine and pestilence in large parts of the third world and refined brutality of commodified existence in the metropolis of the first world, whose technological and cultural sophistication is quite compatible with its growing barbarisation.

Marx had hailed the productive achievements of capitalism. But he had also pointed out the damage capitalism regularly inflicts upon man and nature and warned of its long-term destructive potential. It is this destructive potentiality of capitalism and the threat it poses to human existence on this earth which Rosa Luxemburg later summed up in a prophetic poser: 'socialism or barbarism'. The threat is now becoming daily more real and can well take the form of a nuclear holocaust or an ultimate ecological disaster. Socialism or barbarism are indeed the alternatives for the twenty-first century. If we are unable to build, and build in time, a socialist alternative worthy of the name, what capitalism now promises us is only a future of barbarism. And since the possibility of the destruction our world itself cannot be ruled out, it could well be a future of no future at all. 'History is about the most cruel of all goddesses', Engels had once said. History could now be cruel to us in a way that will really be the 'end of history'. But, as Marxism of Karl Marx has it, nothing is inevitable in human affairs till it happens. We can fight back and reject the future that capitalist masters are making for us. In the final analysis it is how we struggle and fight back that will decide our future. We can still make our future our own way, build it as a society of freedom and equality and a truly rich human life for all – for that is what socialism is about.

Appendix

On the Question of Socialism Today*

It was Engels' adjuration to followers to 'not pick quotations from Marx or from him as if from sacred texts, but think as Marx would have thought in their place.' He had insisted that 'it was only in that sense that the word Marxist had any raison d'etre'.....

Accordingly, I would make a few concluding observations on the question of socialism today, again with the help of passages culled from my *Crisis of Socialism — Notes in Defence of a Commitment*, which carrries a detailed discussion of the issues now being touched upon.

❖

Socialism arose in opposition to capitalism with the rise of modern capitalism itself. Marx's many-sided critique of capitalism soon provide it with a scientific theoretical basis, establishing it as socialism of our times, distiguishing it from its various other forms—some of which (Revolutionary Socialsim, Petty Bourgeois Socialism, German or 'True' Socialism, Conservative or Bourgeois Socialism, Critical Utopian Socialism, etc.) Marx himself noted in the *Communist Manifesto*—

---

* The concluding section of the author's address, 'Future of Socialism', to the journal *Itihasbodh* at Allahabad on March 8, 2007.

forms in which it keeps reappearing from time to time. In other words, socialism came up long before the Soviet Union did, and we are socialist because of capitalism and not because of the Soviet Union. Some of us were in fact socialist despite the Soviet Union. And socialism remains on the agenda of history so long as capitalism lasts.

❖

For Marx socialism is essentially a negation of capitalism, a negation of its economy, politics and ethical-aesthetic values, its multiple alienations and commodification of life. These are no blueprints of socialist society of the future in Marx's social theory. His scientific method forbidding any such speculation, Marx simply refused to 'compose the music of the future'. He visualised the construction of socialism, or communist society proper, as constituting a long period of transition. But the problems of this transition were never seriously discussed or theorised by Marx.

There are only scattered references to it in different writings of Marx and Engels, concerned primarily with characteristics of socialism as a transitional society between capitalism and communism (which they regarded as the goal towards which history was moving). The most important single document of classical Marxism here, that is, on the subject of construction of a new socialist society, is Marx's *Critique of the Gotha Programme*—really Marx's marginal notes to the programme of the German Workers Party, published by Engels after Marx's death, sixteen years after Marx wrote them. The very title is significant. The only time Marx is drawn into making a somewhat detailed, yet all to brief, comment on the subject, it is as a critique of his own party or followers in Germany for their confused and shoddy thinking over several issues, which also included that concerning the socialist society of the future—a critique distinguished for 'the ruthless severity' and 'mercilessness' typical of Marx in matters of theory. To be specifically noted here is that Marx never saw socialism, 'advanced', 'developed', or any other, as a social formation existing in its own right (as Soviet Marxism did); that would be plainly violative of its essential character as Marx defined it, that is a transition between capitalism and communism. As was common in his times, there is a certain loose usage of the term 'socialism' in Karl Marx. Quite often, he used 'socialism' and 'communism' as synonymous terms, both referring to the same kind of society, that is, a 'cooperative society' or 'association' based on 'free associated labour'. More specifically, it is what Marx called 'the first phase of communist society' which later Marxists, including Lenin, came to describe as 'socialism' (as opposed to 'communism' proper). Marx, therefore, nowhere speaks of 'socialism' as a distinct stage or social formation or of 'transition between socialim and communism'. For Marx, as the new society emerges from the capitalist society itself, the former is obviously an integral part of the same new society, being its 'first phase' only chronologically, with the specific kind of developments corresponding to it. For him, between capitalism and communism lies no stage or stages, only a transition, more or less prolonged according to circumstances, possibly a whole epoch or perhaps even more than one historical epoch. Lenin, though sharing the loose usage often equated socialism with communism, was equally explicit in speaking of 'transition period between capitalism and communism'....

I would suggest that Marx's view here is theoretically correct and politically more fruitful as against positing the transition in terms of stages such as 'new democracy', 'people's democracy', a 'revolutionary democracy', 'socialist society', etc.

That there is no fore-ordained model or blueprint of socialism or socialist transition, certainly none suitable for all countries and all times, does not mean absence of general principles that flow from the Marxist tradition, the experience gained in national liberation and social revolutionary struggles and the efforts at socialist construction so far. For this reason, a critical understanding of Marxist tradition and revolutionary struggles of the past, and an equally critical analysis of and drawing of lessons from the past experiments in socialism, even when they have failed, is more than an intellectual game; it is an urgent and practical necessity for socialists everywhere, including those in the third world, seeking a proper perspective on possible socialist transition in their countries....

❖

Socialism, for Marx, is not merely a set of humane economic arrangements; it is *an emancipatory project*. Marx saw socialism in its transition to communism as humankind's transition to 'the realm of freedom' which according to him lies beyond material pursuits, beyond all activity geared to economic needs. He wrote:

> .... The realm of freedom actually begins only where labour which is determined by necessity and mundane considerations ceases; thus *in the very nature of things* it lies beyond the sphere of actual material production. Just as the savage must wrestle with nature to satisfy his wants, to maintain and reproduce life, so must civilised man, and he must do so in all social formations and under all modes of production.... Freedom in this field can only consist in socialised man, the associated producers, rationally regulating their interchange with nature, bringing it under their common control, instead of being ruled by it as by a blind power; and achieving this with the least expenditure of energy and under conditions most favourable to, and worthy of, their human rature. But it nonetheless still remains a realm of necessity. Beyond it begins that development of human power which is an end in itself, the true realm of freedom, which, however, can blossom forth only with this realm of necessity as its basis.

The aspirations of vision that Marx here sets forth is in fact as old as civilisation; it is there, for instance, in Plato and Aristotle, though its realisation, then and afterwards, was seen possible only for a few. Marx put more substance into this aspiration and sought its realisation for all human beings. In other words, economic activity was, throughout, deemed to have meaning only it it serves something other than itself. For Marx this is activities 'valued as an end in theselves' (as he phrased it in the *Grundrisse)*, which for him is indeed 'the true measure of wealth'.....

Marx, in line with his mode of thinking, took a historical view of the growth of needs and desires of human beings as one aspect of the general development of human nature, which is also the subjective aspect of the growth of human powers and capacities. His argument is suggestive of an infinite future of creation and cultivation of 'the wealth of subjective human sensitivity', of specifically human senses, which is really the same as human nature all the time *becoming more human*. And the important point is that, for Marx, the exercise of these naturally and historically produced specifically human senses—the sense for music and poetry, art, science and history, love, justice and compassions, and so on—constituted the very essence of a truly human appropriation of life and nature, a genuinely rich human life. That is how, in pointing out the alienating, depersonalising and dehumanising consequences of capitalism, Marx particularly focused attention of the fact that for all the glorious human senses, whose active and concrete exercise alone constitutes the true content of a genuinely rich human life, capitalism substitutes a single abstract sense, the sense for property, a particular, historically transient, substitute sense which plays havoc with human personality and plunges man, in the words of Ladislav Stoll, 'into the terrible inner sickness of a dehumanised world', Marx wrote: 'In place of all these physical and mental senses there has .... come the sheer estrangement of all these senses—the sense of having. The human being had to be reduced to this absolute poverty in order that he might yield his inner wealth to the outer world'. 'The more you have', said Marx, 'the less you are'. Hence his insistence that 'the transcendence of private property is therefore the complete *emancipation* of all human senses and attributes'. He spoke of communism, 'the actual phase necessary for the next stage of historical development in the process of human emancipation and recovery', 'as the positive transcendence of *private property* as *human self-estrangement*, and therefore as the real *appropriation of the human* essence by and for man; communism therefore as the complete return of man to himself as a social (i.e. human) being—a return become conscious, and accomplished within the entire wealth of previous development'. Marx added: 'What is to be avoided above all is the re-establishing of 'Society' as an abstraction *vis-a-vis* the individual. The individual is the social being. His life.... is therefore an expression and confirmation of *social life'*. Marx is an individualist in the basic sense that his ultimate vision was a society where every individual could be a fully *human* being, where, as Marx himself put it, 'the free development of each is the condition for the free development of all'......

Such is the fulfilment Marx's socialism/communism seeks for humankind. As Engels expressed it, 'it is humanity's leap from the realm of necessity into the realm of freedom', the end of its' pre-history' and beginning of 'truly human history'.

❖

For Marx, socialism is nothing inevitable, it is something to be struggled for.

Marx was no determinist, ever. Whatever determinism there is in his Marxism, is a most conditional one, which accords primacy to human praxis, to revolutionary politics. If attention was drawn to the economic-structural necessities underlying the historical processes, it was for enhancing the freedom for *praxis,* for not foreclosing but liberating human practice, for freer choices by humans, free not in some abstract or metaphysical sense, but in the only possible *human* sense of men and women choosing and acting with the fullest possible knowledge and consideration of the necessities of the objective material situation or circumstances. Such is the dialectics of freedom and necessity in Marx.....

Thus there are no inevitablities in Marx and no guarantees of victory either; only alternatives. Even as he insisted in the *Communist Manifesto* that 'the history of all hitherto existing society is the history of class struggle'. Marx had immediately added that this struggle 'each time ended, either in a revolutionary reconstitution of society at large, or in the common ruin of the contending classes'. Again, he had hailed the productive achievements of capitalism—'it has been the first to show what man's activity can bring about', creating 'more massive and more colossal productive forces than have all preceding generations together' (*Communist Manifesto*). But he had also pointed out not only the damage that capitalism regularly inflicts upon humans and nature but also its long-term destructive potential—'its accumulation process', Marx wrote in *Grundrisse,* can have 'the consequences even for the total destruction of humanity'—a prognosis which Rosa Luxemburg later summed up as the alternative: 'socialism or barbarism'.

Incidentally, these alternatives to socialism—the threat of 'common ruin of the contending classes', and 'the total destruction of humanity' are already a part of the reality of our world today.

❖

For whatever reasons, which certainly included an underestimation of capitalism's productive potential and resilience, Marx gave capitalism a short lease of life, which allowed for the possibility of realising socialism as an emancipatory project, that is initiating the epochal transition this project implied. In his main theory on the subject, based on his view of the historical tendencies of advanced capitalist development in Europe, Marx visualised the necessity as well as the possibility of a transition from capitalism to socialism/communism in the countries of advanced industrial development, with their mature productive basis and proletatian presence—'Empirically, communism is only possible as the act of the dominant peoples "all at once" and simultaneously, which presupposes the universal development of productive forces and the world intercourse bound up with them', is how Marx put it in *The German Ideology*. Accordingly, Marx looked forward to an early revolution in Europe—though he also recognised (in a letter to Engels in 1858): 'For us the difficult question is this: the revolution on the Continent is imminent and its character will be at once socialist; will it not be necessarily crushed in this little corner of the world, since on a much larger terrain the development of bourgeois society is still in the ascendant'. The hoped-for European revolution finally arrived in the aftermath of the first world war but it survived only in Russia, confronting Lenin and his Bolsheviks with a totally unanticipated task: attempt a socialist transition in a single backward country, a situation or possibility that was never theorised by Marx. And now, though not inevitable, the attempt has failed. History seems to have played a trick on the doctrine of Karl Marx. This trick including the failure in the Soviet Union is eminently amendable to explanation in terms of this very doctrine but more important is to note the consequent reality of the contemporary world in relation to Marx's own perspective on socialism and the struggle for socialism in our times.

Of this reality, three features need to be particularly noticed.

First, as a capitalist world, it is a world of 'overdeveloped', 'underdeveloped' or so-called 'developing' countries. The latter two categories are generally well understood but we need to take a closer look at the 'overdeveloped' countries of advanced capitalism. For one, capitalism survives and is indeed dominant today, but as noticed earlier, it remains a failed system. Other considerations apart, capitalism has been a failure in terms of possibly the most legitimate criteria for assessing the performance of a social system: 'fullness of employment' and 'goodness of employment' of the actual and potential resources available in society. Never before in human history has the gap between society's potentiality and society's performance been so immense as it is today is capitalism's current stage of development. Evidence is there, as we have already noticed, in the extraordinary productive capacity that three successive industrial revolutions have put at the disposal of humankind and the poverty and illiteracy, squalid slums and homelessness that are the lot of millions of families in the wealthiest countries of the capitalist world and the hunger and misery of hundreds of millions of people, living out their empty and barren lives in the hovels of the peripheral or semi-peripheral poor countries of the third world....

Capitalism continues to survive but this by itself, cannot be seen as an argument for the desirability, or a sign of the progressiveness of the capitalist order, much less as any sort of 'triumph' of capitalism. 'That position', says Paul Baran, 'is no more defensible than would be the view that an inability of the human body to resist tuberculosis, however caused, furnishes a proof of the harmlessness or even usefulness of that illness'....

He adds: 'The failure of an irrationally organised society to generate internal forces pressing towards and resulting in its abolition and replacement by more rational, more humane social relations results necessarily in economic stagnation, cultural decay, and a widespread sense of despondency. Such a society—

even if once the most advanced in the world—loses its position of leadership, slides into the backwaters of historical development, and turns into a breeding ground of reaction inhumanity, and obscurantism.' This is indeed the case today, not only in the United States but increasingly in the other so-called advanced societies of late capitalism....

The US leading, these societies are, in a profound sense, to a greater or lesser degree, sick societies. Concerned scholars have written of the phenomenon of 'alienation' in these societies, their citizens' growing sense of anomie and estrangement, of isolation, hostility and frustration. They are sick with these and a hundred other social and psychic ailments born of prolonged living under an essentially irational system, sick with apathy and boredom, with 'other-directedness' and conformism, with fears, insecurities and neuroses of all kinds. Their sustained social regression is reflected as much in the reaction and obscurantism they breed, their frivolous consumption and culture of drugs, and even guns, as in the debilitating barrage of fraudulent politics, barren culture and stupefying entertainment, inspirational rackets and demoralising press, and comic books, to which their people, even otherwise ill-educated, are exposed all the time. Societies in the grip of crises which they cannot resolve, they are inevitably producing deep pathological deformations which manifest themselves variously in different places as racism, sexism, anti-Semitism, xenophobia, ethnic or national hatred, fundamentalism and intolerance, even as plain cruelty and aggression. Poverty, unemployment and insecurity-related crimes and associated phenomena—ill health and suicides, alcoholism and drug addiction, racist discrimination and criminal violence, violence against women and child abuse, etc.—are on the rise everywhere. In many of these 'advanced' societies, marginal indigenous populations are rapidly being wiped out for one reason or another. By their very nature, profoundly immoral societies, based as they are on domination and exploitation of man by man, along with humanistic values and culture and all human relationships, even their professed moralities and principles now stand devastated by the morality and values of 'the market'. And, most significantly, there is the near-absence of ideals in these societies, of any concern for a better future to strive for, that has been the motive force of all human progress in the past. The instruments of communication and discovery invented by their technological genius have become the means of debasing people's understanding and preventing them from looking beyond the capitalist horizon....

Indeed, the sickness of these so-called advanced societies, the spiritual disarray of the capitalist civilisation they represent, is nowhere more evident than in their cynical idealisation of capitalism as it exists and utter lack of any vision of a s secure and more satisfying life beyond their 'consumerist heaven of instant gratification', a life which would be satisfactory of basic human needs—decent livelihood, knowledge, solidarity, cooperation with fellow human beings, gratification in work and freedom from toil—and provide the possibility of men and women appropriating the world with all their glorious *human* senses. It needs to be added that these societies are all the more sick societies because they need to change the existing state of affairs but are unable to generate the necessary social forces for carrying out the revolutionary change they so badly need.....

The continuance of capitalism as 'sick' societies of advanced capitalist West has an important implication. In a sense socialism arrived a little before its time, attempted as it was first in Russia, a society that was not prepared to build it. The Bolsheviks had to contend with the problems of a backward, underdeveloped capitalist-feudal social order, problems which caused grave distortions and contributed to the ultimate failure of their attempt to build socialism. Those who may be called upon to build a late-arrived socialism in advanced capitalist countries will have to contend with equally difficult but *different* problems of an 'overdeveloped' capitalism—a capitalism living beyond its time as it were, beyond the period of its historical legitimacy. In other words, as with 'underdevelopment', 'overdevelopment' too poses its own unanticipated problems for the realisation of Marx's project of socialism.

Socialism, of course, remains on the agenda wherever capitalism exists, be it 'overdeveloped', 'underdeveloped', 'developing' or any other. And there is always the overarching question as to what kind of society we, as human beings, want to have. Surely it is people and not 'economic growth' or productivity that must come first in such a society. It has to be a humane society that fosters cooperation, solidarity and respect for universal ethical values, and makes for a non-alienated, 'truly rich human life' that Marx spoke of. Of course, such a society is impossible without basic material security and need satisfaction. But to believe that you can assure need satisfaction through greed, private acquisitive drives, universal competition and strife—the values of capitalism—and yet hope for a humane society of cooperation and solidarity is utopianism of the worst kind. Subordinating humanity to economics, to imperatives of the market, capitalism commodifies life and undermines and rots away the relations between human beings which constitute societies. Its ethos of the marketplace—competition, egoism, aggression, alienation, universal venality, in short the rat race—creates a moral vacuum in which nothing counts except what the individual wants and can grab, here and now. At the end of it all, even when wants are satisfied, the people are ever more subordinated, ever less free, ever more flattened and made passive by the dictatorship of consumerism, that arbitratily shapes values, imposing on them the heavy burden of uniformity. The values of difference, individualisation (not individualism), all-sided development of man, of human freedom itself, disappear in the marketplace which is proclaimed to the free. As human beings, people simply don't fit into capitalism, which is a quintessential market society. For a truly humane society to come into existence, capitalism has to go....

But, in view of their 'overdeveloped', 'underdeveloped' or 'developing' character, to speak of socialism in relation to these capitalist societies is not to posit socialism as achievable today or tomorrow, or even the day after, but to posit it as people's alternative strategic goal, as the principle governing people's politics which links together their immediate, ongoing and emerging struggles in an ultimate specifics and speed will depend on the objective material conditions and the nature and balance of class forces involved at each stage of the struggle .....

In other words, while expressions like 'building socialism'

or 'building socialism of the 21st century' have a certain historical and political legitimacy, what is on the agenda is a *socialism-oriented development,* such that, no matter how slow or halting or contradictions-laden, it is a development away from capitalism and the imperatives of its market and *towards* Marx's emancipatory vision of socialism, which, in any case, was visualised as a transition spanning an entire epoch even more than one epoch.

This, again, is not to suggest any 'model' of socialist politics. Just as there is no single or foreordained model of socialism, one that is suitable for all climes and all times, there is none of socialist politics either. The specific conditions or demands and the forms of struggle they generated will vary from country to country. Which however, does not mean the absence of general principles to guide it that flow from the Marxist tradition and the experience gained in social revolutionary and national liberation struggles. The recovery of these principles is in fact a must for any successful pursuit of socialist politics today ....

Second, since global capitalism is nationally organised and immediately dependent on national states, national economies and national states remain the primary terrain of anit-capitalist organisation and struggle. Of course, an international perspective, working people's solidarity across national frontiers, remains vital to any socialist movement. And today there exists a focus for such solidarity as has, perhaps, never before existed in the history of capitalism. The universalisation of capitalism has not brought about the cessation but instead the universalisation of struggle against capitalism. When, with globalisation, just about every state is following the same destructive logic, domestic struggles against that common logic can be the basis—in fact the strongest possible basis—of a new internationalism. But looking for that internationalism must not be an excuse for giving up on local national struggles. The main arenas of struggle against global capitalism still remain local and national. 'Workers of all countries, unite' remains the motto but this 'unity' obviously begins at home. There is a growing space for common transnational struggles, but the established order has still to be primarily fought on our own home pitch. As the *Manifesto* put it a long time ago: 'the proletariat of each country must, of course, first of all settle matters with its own bourgeoisie.' If the historical experience of more than a century since the Paris Commune is any guide this is exactly how it has been. The world revolutionary process has turned out to be extremely uneven and has moved from country to country.....

In other words, the nation state is indeed the concrete terrain on which the struggle for the radical transformation of society must begin and may have to be carried forward. It may be added that to argue that a nation state—and this includes states of the size and resources of Britain, France or Italy, or for that matter, India, China or Russia—cannot provide the ground on which the radical transformation of society can be attempted is to rule out such a transition for the forthcoming historical period. It is to abdicate the struggle for socialism in our time......

Third, it was Marx's prognosis that capitalism in its ultimate consequences could spell even 'the total destruction of humanity'. But, giving capitalism a short lease of life, Marx never explored this distant possibility. The distant possibility is now an imminent threat hanging over the future of humankind. As noted earlier, Rosa Luxemburg had summed up Marx's prognosis in her famous poser 'socialism or barbarism'. Capitalism living beyond its historical time indeed spells a future of barbarism for humankind. It could be a nuclear holocaust that its politics has threatened for more than half a century of the almost certai ecological disaster which—noise over so-called 'sustainable development' notwithstanding—capitalism's accumulative logic now portends. This makes the struggle for socialism all the more imperative and urgent today.

❖

It can be legitimately argued, without any underestimation of the prospects of socialist renewal in the advanced capitalist West or the erstwhile 'socialist world', that it is the countries of the third world which are likely to be the storm centres of such struggle, keeping socialism still on the agenda for the future of humankind. For the simple reason that they have no other choice, the common people there have no future otherwise. For the same reasons as in the past, the world revolutionary process is more likely to proceed through the backward, 'less developed' or 'developing' countries of the periphery and semi-periphery of the world capitalist system ....

Therefore, a couple of additional observations on the question of struggle for socialism in these countries will not be out of place.

As a result of the unequal development in capitalist expansion, for causes that are neither local nor conjunctural but systemic and structural to capitalism as a world system, socialist revolutions or revolutionary movements of our time have appeared most often not at the centre but at the periphery of world capitalism—in Russia, China, Cuba, Indo-China, or in the name of socialism, Asia, Africa, and Latin America. For this is indeed where the worst victims of global capitalism's irrationality and exploitation are to be found, and therefore from where the challenge to capitalism emanated. The collapse of the Soviet Union does not end or modify the structural logic of global capitalism as manifested in poverty, underdevelopment, deindustrialisation and exploitation in Asia, Africa, and Latin America. It has only made global capitalism all the more powerful and given a new edge to its predatory logic. Any social system built on inequality in the command of human and natural resources works in many ways to reproduce itself and to increase the extent of the in-built inequality. So does capitalism. But as a market-governed system, capitalism carries this process to the extremes. The law of accumultion of capital inexorably produces, reproduces, and enhances inequality—wealth at one end and poverty at the other, not only within countries but on a world scale. And this is precisely what *globalisation*—another of the currently fashionable, reality-obscuring buzzwords—does. It has only sharpened the global capitalism's contradiction between its developed centre and exploited periphery. But this, if the past is any guide, also makes this periphery, the third world of the worst victims of contemporary capitalism, the site of revolts, of new countrywide challenges to the global capitalist order, of the resumed struggle for socialism....

This, as mentioned earlier, is not to posit socialism as achievable today or tomorrow, or even the day after, but to posit it as people's alternative strategic goal, as the principle governing people's politics which links together their immediate, ongoing and emerging struggles in an ultimate project of revolutionary transformation of society, as the goal of a long transitional process whose specifics and speed will depend on the objective material conditions and the nature and balance of class forces involved at each stage of the struggle for the socialist goal. Immediately it means saying 'no' to globalisation, a 'delinking' from the global capitalist market—which however does not mean any kind of 'autarky'—and opting for a pro-people socialism-oriented autonomous development, one governed not by external imperatives, those flowing from the requirements of the world capitalist market (export-led growth, etc.) and the associated consumerism of the rich, but primarily by *internal* imperatives, those flowing from an assessment of country's own resources and the needs of its people. Development which can meet the material needs of the people in the third world is impossible within the framework of capitalism, national or globalised. Socialism has to be the strategic goal, whatever be the long or short transitional route to it. Historical experience allows no other choice....

Any attempt at saying 'no' to globalisation or 'delinking' is likely to exact a heavy price in many ways, including an unavoidable trade-off between the requirements of productivity and those of minimising the polarising impact of global capitalism's enourmous economic power. But once 'productivism' is abandoned and human welfare has the priority, this need not be a deterrent to adopting the strategy that 'delinking' involves. The details of economic policies in pursuit of this strategy will obviously vary from country to country. Here only a few broadly suggestive observations can be made.....

This strategy postulates a revolutionary state, representative of a popular front of workers and peasants, undertaking at the very outset a comprehensive programme of eradication of mass poverty, universal primary education, healthcare, housing, and provision of basic necessities for all. Initiating steps towards redistribution of incomes and development of backward areas will be a priority for state's active intervention in the economy which, even as it covers such areas as foreign relations, production and social distribution, research and training, and the like, will need to secure an effective transitional combination of planning and market forces without letting the market or its values take over. Agrarian revolution benefiting the rural proletariat and small farmers, thereby improving the productive capacity in the rural areas, and laying the basis of cooperative effort and voluntary collectivisation of agriculture should be high on its agenda of economic reconstruction, as should be the transformation of the informal sector into a popularly managed transitional economy. A building up or restructuring of industry is obviously necessary. But it can neither be one based on 'international competitiveness' (that is promoting exports through low costs of local labour) nor on 'import substitution' (promoting production for the consumption of the privileged local classes). Not that all effort in these directions is ruled out; some of it may even be necessary. Only priorities, for years to come, lie elsewhere. The important thing is to develop and organise productive forces in a manner that helps the rural sector leap forward, carries industrialisation to the countryside and in general ensures a pattern of growth which, refusing the wasteful production to satisfy elite consumerism, immediately benefits the popular masses, satisfying their basic needs, needs created and satisfiable by the redistribution of income. It should be obvious that the overall development of a third world country today cannot support the first world consumption levels of its elites. What is needed is a diversification and development of internal markets for domestic goods and services governed by the overall priciple that, beyond a certain necessary priority charges of an unequal nature, private needs and wants should be satisfied (and this goes for their increasing satisfaction) only at a level at which they can be satisfied for all, and beyond this all increase in the production of consumer goods should be for collective consumption....

Such a socialism oriented pro-people endogenous development process will draw on its own strengths and domestic resources and capacities, including those of the hardworking poor who yet remain the most creative ane productive force in society. It will give the common people, an overwhelming mass of workers and peasants, a positive stake in the economy and mobilise them for building a better society as well as for the inevitable struggle against global imperialism and its local allies or partners—an awakened and aroused people are indeed the best defence even against armed aggression. Needless to add, such popular mobilisation and struggle will be all the time necessary to carry through the strategic option that socialism-oriented delinking involves....

What the above strategy in effect demands is that not economics but politics, that is class politics, is put in command of the economy. 'Politics in command' means posing such questions as: growth? but which growth? for what purpose? for whose sake, whose benefit or profit? for what kind of society and within which environment? These are questions which are central to any search for a real alternative to capitalism, vital for the very survival of socialist movement today. They are all the more vital to pose in the third world suffering the worst ravages of capitalism. We must ask: is our goal meeting 'the needs of the economy', its 'anonymous masters' as they have been called—'abstractions such as financial markets, interest rates, exchange rates, commodity prices, indexes and statistical artefacts of all kinds'—or satisfaction of the needs of the people, allowing citizens the possibility of living as human beings? Is the starting point of our economic exercises to be calculation of deficits in order to cut them at the cost of the people or a determination of resources needed to satisfy people's needs in order to find or raise them? And our language? Do we practise the obscurantism of GDP, fiscal and revenue deficits, balance or payments, growth rates, etc., or speak more humanely in terms of such things as food and clean drinking water, health care and sanitation, housing and education, etc. so that economy becomes a transparent and accountable means of integrating these basic human needs of the people with a planned use of domestic resources, an use which also takes care of questions of equality, social justice including gender justice, employment, ecologically sustainable development, etc.?...

Economic and technological backwardness is often presssed as an argument to counter the plea for such autonomous economic development. (Getting access to the most modern technology is another usual argument for the need to actively participate in world trade). This calls for two very brief observations. In the first place it is useful to recognise that if, despite economic backwardness, the priority is given to the needs of the poorest and most deprived sections of the people, there is much that can be done at the outset even in absence of growth of productive forces. The redistribution of wealth and the use of idle or under-utilised human and material resources, their more productive deployment, can bring quick improvement in health, education and general living conditions of large masses of people. Early years of post-revolutionary societies in the Soviet Union and elsewhere provide ample evidence of this achievement which could be the basis for further development along socialist lines.

In the second place, once we overcome the fetishism of science and technology—which attributes to them properties or power they do not possess, and at times even expects them to do the job of a social revolution which they simply cannot—and, as with economic development so with technology, ask the basic question: 'technology for what purpose?', the argument for getting access to the most modern Western technology via globalisation—even if that was certain which it most certainly is not—loses much of its force. If the purpose is to satisfy the consumerist hunger of the privileged part of the population and therefore supply it with the most modern gadgets, designs, and goodies of the West, then rushing into globalisation is indeed understandable. But if the purpose or priority is to meet the needs of all the people for decent food, clothing and shelter, clean water, proper sanitation and health protection, education and cultural opportunities and the like, then devoting scarce resources to the most modern technology will be only wasteful because there is little in the latest technology of the West that would make a significant contribution. Infact what is most useful and relevant in technology, western or otherwise, for improving the way of life of the masses is widely known. Most of this technology is already available at home and what else is needed is obtainable in the normal course of managed trade....

❖

My observations so far are directly or indirectly relevant to the struggle for socialism in India. But, exemplified by the crises of CPM politics in West Bengal, the issue of this struggle has also come up, in a *sui generis* form, at the level of state politics in India which calles for a brief discussion in its own right.

Our struggle for freedom was a struggle to break out of a globalisation whose structural logic meant wealth in England and poverty in India. This was a necessary, though not sufficient, condition to be able to build a better life for our people. Aware of this exploitative logic of the global capitalist market, of centuries of experience of imperialism which provides little evidence of the beneficial effect of foreign investment in countries of the third world so far as the common people are concerned, and in its own way influenced by the interim successes of the Soviet Union, the post-independence (Nehruvian) national project opted for the strategic goal of a state-led self-reliant development promising economic growth with 'equity and distributive justice' to the people. For understandable reasons, it did not work out as Nehru had intended. There was a degree of economic growth but not much equity or distributive justice for the people and the project ended up building an India-specific government-supported third worldist capitalism. The rhetoric of 'socialistic pattern of society' only deceived the people, legitimised the statist capitalism that was coming up and created confusion about it as 'socialism' so that when, passing through a series of economic and political crises mid-1960s onward, the project finally collapsed in 1991, it was, and continues to be, misinterpreted as the failure of socialism in India.

The post-independence national project having collapse, 1991 onwards, India's ruling classes, through their different political formations, notably, the Congress and the BJP, have gone in for 'globalisation' as their new strategic option—a shift from the state-supported capitalism to a wholly privatised 'free market' capitalism and from self-reliance in economic development to reliance on Foreign Direct Investment and the multinationals, a shift euphemistically described as 'economic reforms' which has little to offer to the common Indian people. The much-touted 'growth rates' are no indication of general well-being in a capitalist society and the so-called 'trickle down', if and when it occurs, is no better than feeding horses with oats so that something passes down to the road for the sparrows, as Galbraith once described it. Over the past decade-and-a-half or so, whatever be the benefits 'economic reforms' has brought to a small section at the top, it has further polarised our society, played havoc with the lives of our common people and pushed them still further into a peripheralised existence within the global capitalist system.

This is nothing surprising. 'Economic reforms' is only a euphemism for capitalist development whose structural logic, as a former President of Brazil once reported it to the masters in Washington, is : 'the economy is doing fine, the people are not.' A market-governed economic growth simply cannot deliver 'inclusive growth', to use another of the proliferating buzz words of our time. Instead, it is by its vary nature exculusionary, and the logic of the market, with its inevitable winners and losers, only makes for 'the secession of the successful', as the economist Robert Reich once phrased it. One look at their economic policies or concerns, their lifestyles and values will reveal how far 'the successful' of India's marketplace have already 'seceded' from the vast majority of their supposedly 'unsuccessful' follow countryman.

Pointing out that 'the unprecedented high economic growth on which privileged India prides itself is a measure of the high speed at which India of privilege is distancing itself from the India of crushing poverty (and that) the higher the rate of economic growth along this pattern becomes, the greater would be the underdevelopment of India', Amit Bhaduri has written: 'Destruction of livelihoods and displacement of the poor in the name of industrialisation, big dams of power generation and irrigation, corporatisation of agriculture despite farmers' suicides, modernization and beautification of our cities by demolishing slums are showing everyday how development can turn perverse.... The devil in angel's guise would soon appear when large populations in rural India would be rendered landless, jobless, homeless, incomeless, rootless and displaced making way for gragantuan SEZs, the so-called epitomes of economic development.'

This raises what I have elsewhere described as 'contemporary India's most important *unraised* political question', the question of a people's strategic option, an alternative path of development distinct from and in opposition to that of India's ruling classes. The absence of this option, an alternative path of development, which can only be a socialism-oriented autonomous development, is the tragedy of the Left in India, part of the larger tragedy of the Indian people today.

And this is where lie the roots of the current crisis or tragedy of the CPM politics in West Bengal. That is how, despite its 30 odd years of uninterrupted power in the state, the CPM has not been able to project the image of doing something *significantly* different from or better than what is happening in other states; instead, operating on the terrain of bourgeois politics, responding to issues it presents and accepting the choice it offers, has entailed a corruption of consciousness and loss of revolutionary commitment. Criticism of bourgeois parties for failing by their own standards and programmes—a staple of parliamentary politics—has led to the CPM endorsing these standards and programmes itself so that its own original concerns have come to be given a go-by. And now, to the adulation of the corporate world and ridicule of the bourgeois media, West Bengal, like the other states, often in competition with them, has chosen to tread the centre-decreed neo-liberal, that is capitalist path of development. Left rhetoric apart, the only difference is that, possibly because the communists, unlike others, take theory—no matter what it is—seriously, their government alone, in its pursuit of this path (its corporate-led industrialisation and Special Economic Zones) has gone in for a shooting spree against the people!

The best of official defence is in terms of 'the role of a Left-ruled state government in a situation when the Centre has embraced neo-liberal polities'; 'The state governments', we are told, 'function within severe constraints. The simplistic notion that the West Bengal, Kerala and Tripura governments can adopt an alternative model to the Centre's policies has to be dispelled.' At its worst there is unqualified justification and advocacy of neo-liberal policies, the corporate-ed industrialisation and Special Economic Zones. As this 'defence' is repeated by one Party leader or ideologue after another, one is reminded of the 'secondary illiterates' that poet Hans Magnus Enzensberger has spoken of—those who had the benefit of literacy once and come to know a few things, know them to be true, but now, gone illiterate, have forgotten whatever they once knew. (The tribe of 'secondary illiterates', in a truly rich variety, is growing and prospering outside the CPM too, if the media, especially TV, its talk shows, 'debates' and 'big fights' are any indication).

Capitalism is today so powerful and pervasive as to have become invisible, and it is all the more powerful for being invisible. You no longer see or recognise it, even refer to by its proper name. Thus it is 'globalisation', 'neo-liberalism' or 'liberalisation', 'structural adjustment', 'new economic policy', 'economic reforms' (and now with the CPM joining in) 'industrialisation', 'development and progress', even 'civilisation'—that is anything but capitalism. If you cannot even *see or think* capitalism you obviously cannot argue or act against it. And it capitalism is not recognised, its negation, socialism too disappears from your theory and practice. CPM leaders no longer speak in the language of socialism or class politics, not in public at least, not even when bourgeois ideologues of TV anchores get provocatively aggressive. And on the rare occasions they refer to Marxism, only vulgarise it. Here is a gem of a vulgarisation from Buddhadeb Bhattacharjee, Chief Minister of West Bengal: 'From agriculture to industry, from villages to cities, this is civilisation. We Marxists never deny this aim. We too want this to happen'. One again recalls Hans Magnus Enzensberger. This time his moving short peom, *Karl Heinrich Marx*:

> I see you betrayed
> by your disciples
> only your enemies
> remained what they were.

Let me cut this dismal story short and speak of what the situation demands and what needs to be done. The situation demands that we return to calling things by their proper names and that right questions be asked if right answers are to be had. In other words, 'economic reforms' has a proper name, capitalist development, which, therefore, has to be rejected by communists or socialists at both national and state or local levels; and the question to be asked is: what can be done and what should not be done in West Bengal in the light of socialist principles? The need is to mobilise all the available resources within and without the Left parties to work out an answer to this question, that is, a programme of possible alternative socialism-oriented policies for the state. The resources are there, among them the Left's own mass base and organisations, the state's revolutionary traditions, a significant section of supportive intelligentsia and what Victor G. Kiernan has called 'mankind's moral reserves, its accumulation of moral capital', which socialism as an ideal can legitimately claim for itself and bank on. Socialism today, more than ever before has the potential to be 'a movement of immense majority in the interest of immense majority' as *Communist Manifesto* had proclaimed. Whole areas—education, healthcare, people's empowerment, ethical governance, environment, the closed down or locked out factories in urban areas, the stalled land reforms in rural areas and poverty and hunger in both places—are crying out for possible socialism-oriented initiatives in the state. The question is really of priorities, of putting politics, that is class politics in command and making socialism-inspired choices. The CPM itself could do with some socialism-inspired rectification.

It is not for me to suggest any concrete policies. This is best done by the people of West Bengal, its workers, peasants and the allied intelligentsia. I will only share a few general considrations. Primarily relevant at the national level, these considerations are not without their relevance for policies at the state or local levels.

The concept of 'development' is by nature ideological, suggestive of something desirable, involving 'the overarching question' I have raised and answered earlier, as to what kind of society we as human beings want to have. And the answer holds even for our poor and backward people. With its subordination of humanity to economy, and the consequent commodification of life, its ethos of greed, private acquisitive drives, egoism and aggression, competition and strife, in short rat race, its 'pseudo-moral principles', as Keynes once put it, 'which have hag-ridden us for 200 years (and) by which we have exalted some of the most distasteful of human qualities into the position of the highest virtues', and its production process which, as Marx said, turns worker into 'an automatic motor of a fractional operation' and 'cripples his body and mind', capitalist society is not the society we want to have. However poor or backward today, we need to *move away* from capitalism-oriented development and, however slowly or falteringly, *move towards* building a humane, socialist society, that fosters equality, cooperation, solidarity and respect for universal ethical values.

Again, 'development' is not synonymous with capitalist development, nor industrialisation ipso facto industrialisation sponsored by the private sector, corporate or any ohter. Nor is it that industrial activities are a natural monopoly of private entities, domestic or foreign. These are all ideology-determined positions, bearing witness to the hegemonic control of boureois ideology in our society these days. Historical experience makes it abundantly clear that paths of development other than the capitalist path are possible and there can be varieties of ways of industrialisation. For example, under the aegis of public or cooperative sectors, or as 'a programme of decentralised, employment intensive rural industrialisation through participatory democracy at the local level'.

The public sector *by itself* has no socialist implications. But it remains a serious industrialisation and employment option. Leave aside it successes elesewhere, even in India, the public sector has not been the kind of failure bourgeois ideologues make it out to be. There are, 'the stunning achievements of the National Thermal Power Corporation, Bharate Heavy Electricals, Nalco, the Oil and Natural Gas Commission, the Gas Authority of India or the Indian Oil Corporation' as a knowledgeable scholar has recently pointed out. And even the failure of public sector in India, such as it has been, is better understood as the failure of Indian democracy whence alone correctives to its malfunctioning or failure could have come, unlike the private sector where correctives come from the market, though often needing to be backed by the state. Therefore, the answer to this failure is a differently working democracy, an effective exercise of people's power in the state, and not a market-based private sector with its record of now well established worse failures.

As for corporate-led industrialisation being an answer to the problem of unemployment, such industrialisation generally does not generate much employment. Even as it simultaneously destroys employment in activities supplanted by it and its offshoots, its primary concern with profit-making involves cutting costs including labour costs. It is indeed an illusion that corporate industrialisation with its labour-saving automated technologies can ever generate net employment opportunities. As to the promise of 'indirect' employment created in the wake of industry, it has been well-described as 'a pie in the sky for the peasants'. Above and beyond all this is the overarching issue of the *quantity and even more quality of employment* in this age of globalisation, with its 'jobless growth', ruthless competition in the markets at home and abroad, and vast masses of our people reduced to be 'the reserve army of labour' for national and global capitalism.

Yet again: that the initial modern economic and industrial development, that in the west, occurred in the capitalist form is no reason to believe that this is the only way it can take place. Marx, who studied and theorised this development, certainly did not think so. In his now well-known letter to the editorial board of the Russian periodical, *Otechestvenniye Zapiski,* in response to a critic, 'honouring me too much' as he said, Marx specifically disowned any claims of having provided a 'master key' or 'universal passport' of 'a general historico-philosophical theory, the supreme virtue of which consists in being super-historical'. Rejecting the very notion of such a theory, he insisted that Capital contained 'my historical sketch of the genesis of capitalism in Western-Europe' and it must not be metamorphosed into 'an historic-philosophic theory of the general path every people is fated to tread, whatever the historical circumstances in which it finds itself'.......

Later, apropos of the possible historical options for Russia, Marx wrote of 'the finest chance ever offered by history to a people' to pass directly from a feudal to a communist phase of development. Marx believed that it could, provided there was an early revolution in Russia, early enough to save the peasant commune from being destroyed. Marx specifically distanced himself from his 'disciples' in Russia, Plekhanov and others, whose strictly evolutionist Marxism saw history as constituted by necessary stages and postulated the necessity of a capitalist stage in Russia's advance to socialism. Marx found their doctrines 'boring' and referred to them deriseively as 'Russian capitalism admirers'. Marx's position also involved a new recognition of the great revolutionary potential of the peasantry.......

I may add that historical experience of construction of socialism in the Soviet Union, during the Mao years in China and now in Cuba, more than validates the view that economic development including industrialisation along other than the capitalist path is possible.

I would here also like to reproduce a couple of passages from Marx and Engels which are in their own way relevant to the context of the issue under discussion. The passages from Marx relate to the Marxist concept of 'primitive accumulation of capital.'

> The capitalist system presupposes the complete separation of the labourers from all property in the means by which they can realise their labour... a process that transforms, on the one hand, the social means of subsistence and of production into capital, on the other, the immediate producers into wage labourers. This historical process... appears as primitive, because it form the pre-historic stage of capital....

Most basic in this process are

> those moments when great masses of men are suddenly and forcibly torn from their means of subsistence, and hurled as free

> and 'unattached' proletarians on the labour market... law itself becomes... the instrument of the theft of the people's land... The history of this expropriation, in different countries, assumes different aspects, and runs through its various phases in different orders of succession, and at different periods.

The passage from Engels deals with the question of 'small peasantry':

> What, then, is our attitude towards the small peasantry? How shall we have to deal with it on the day of our accession to power?... we foresee the inevitable doom of the small peasant, but .... it is not our mission to hasten it by any interference on our part.
>
> Secondly, it is just as evident that when we are in possession of state power, we shall not even think of forcibly expropriating the small peasants (regardless of whether with or without compensation), as we shall have to do in the case of the big landowners. Our task relative to the small peasant consists, in the first place, in effecting a transition of his private enterprise and private possession to cooperative ones, not forcibly but by dint of example and the proffer of social assistance for this purpose...
>
> We, of course, are decidedly on the side of the small peasant; we shall do everything at all permissible to make his lot more bearable, to facilitate his transition to the cooperative should he decide to do so, and even to make it possible for him to remain on his small holding for a protracted length of time to think the matter over, should he still be unable to bring himself to this decision.
>
> We do this not only because we consider the small peasant living by his own labour as virtually belonging to us, but also in the direct interest of the Party. The greater the number of peasants whom we can save from being actually hurled down into the proletariat, whom we can win to our side while they are still peasants, the more quickly and easily the social transformation will be accomplished.

Worker-peasant alliance was always at the core of revolutionary politics in Marx and Lenin.

Finally, there is the consideration that backwardness, such as there is, is not without its advantages. To put it most briefly, we can learn from the past experience with economic development, avoid its negative consequences, for example, the damage that capitalist development regularly inflicts upon human beings and natural environment. We can avoid the supposedly Marxist fascination with 'development of productive forces' that characterised the erstwhile 'socialist' economies and the obsession with 'economic growth' that plagues a capitalist economy. We can better negotiate the necessary trade-offs between economic development and social justice, between requirements of productivity or efficiency and environmental sustainability or quality life which is not entirely a matter of material progress or economic growth. In other words, our backwardness gives us the opportunity 'to do something new', the all-important option of a path of development which, subordinating economy to humanity, plans and develops it in a way that is, in Marx's word, 'worthy of our human nature'.

To conclude: it is simply inconceivable that there can ever be a situation where socialist principles do not indicate what can be done and what should not be done in the light of these principles. With politics, that is class politics in command, socialism-oriented initiatives are indeed possible at the state and local levels in the Left-ruled states. The need is for the CPM to mobilise all the resources within and without the Left parties to work out an alternative path of development geared to the strategic goal of socialism, implement whatever part of it is implementable at the state and local levels in the states where the Left is in power, and mobilise the people elsewhere for it with primacy given to extra-parliamentary struggles. This will make the Left-ruled states an example for the rest of the country and help the Party and the Left to rally all the radical forces in the country—NAPM, ultra-Left formations, militant NGOs, etc.—to emerge as a genuine and effective alternative to the ruling class class politics at the centre, with its own agenda of pro-people, self-realiant socialism-oriented development for the country. Of course, it is going to be a long haul and we don't have to mix up our own mortality with a time-table for the achievement of socialist goals.

But then, perhaps, it is too much or too late for the CPM to make a principled Marxist response to the situation it faces.

Some time back, in a critical comment on CPM's lack of a

strategic goal, distinct from and opposed to that of the ruling classes, and its pursuit or neo-liberal policies in West Bengal, I had written:

> May be the Bhattacharjee turn in CPM politics signals that the old fire gone, happily 'in power' (rather quarantined) in its three States, the party, 'changes' and 'reformed' by its Bhattacharjees, no longer 'dreams' or thinks in Marxist or Leninst ways. 'One residual consequence of the Soviet collapse', I have noted elsewher, 'is the sudden inhibition of social imagination.' May be, like so many other Communists and Socialists, the CPM too has gone 'ralist' and finally succembed to this inhibition. It may even be that the party does not hope of ever being in power at Delhi with its own agenda, and, unable or unwilling 'to do something new' that the situation demands, it ses its future as a pro-people pressure group at the Centre and the best manager of 'economic reforms' in the States. There is plenty of room for such social democratic politics in our country today. And, as that 'most ambitious and intransigent theorisation of ultra-capitalism as a global order', Thomas Friedman's *The Lexus and the Olive Tree* has sloganised: 'one dare not be a globaliser today without being a social democrat'!

But I had then added:

> Sad about the situation one hopes that these 'may bes' are not yet a reality with the entire leadership of the CPM, that the party retains enough of Marxism and revolutionary commitment to keep its original promise to the India people.

Today, while sadness persists and hope has continued to dwindle, a possibility threatens which critics on the Left, including the ultra-Left, themselves unable to develop a genuine alternative to ruling class economics and politics, need to take serious note of. The policies and politics currently pursued by the CPM in West Bengal may well lead to its disintegration and decline as any kind of Left force in Indian politics. And this will be yet another tragedy for our long-suffering people.

Index

INDEX OF NAMES

INDEX OF SUBJECTS